Pedagogy
PRIMER

PETER LANG
New York • Washington, D.C./Baltimore • Bern
Frankfurt am Main • Berlin • Brussels • Vienna • Oxford

Philip M. Anderson

Pedagogy PRIMER

PETER LANG
New York • Washington, D.C./Baltimore • Bern
Frankfurt am Main • Berlin • Brussels • Vienna • Oxford

Library of Congress Cataloging-in-Publication Data

Anderson, Philip M.
Pedagogy primer / Philip M. Anderson.
p. cm. — (Peter Lang primers)
Includes bibliographical references and index.
1. Education—United States.
2. Teaching—United States. I. Title.
LA217.2.A53 371.102—dc22 2008039580
ISBN 978-1-4331-0044-4 (hardcover)
ISBN 978-0-8204-8140-1 (paperback)

Bibliographic information published by **Die Deutsche Bibliothek**.
Die Deutsche Bibliothek lists this publication in the "Deutsche Nationalbibliografie"; detailed bibliographic data is available on the Internet at http://dnb.ddb.de/.

Cover design by Clear Point Designs

The paper in this book meets the guidelines for permanence and durability of the Committee on Production Guidelines for Book Longevity of the Council of Library Resources.

29 Broadway, 18th floor, New York, NY 10006
www.peterlang.com

Printed in the United States of America

Contents

A Note to the Reader

A careful reader will no doubt perceive some repetition in the following chapters. An analytical or logical reader, or someone committed to modern notions of textual efficiency, will wonder if this is an error on the author's part. This repetition is not unconscious, unintentional, or a mistake. A pedagogical text should reflect the structure of its topic and attempt to demonstrate some of its principles. Repetition is necessary to teach concepts, which are complex ideas that require multiple contexts, different lenses, and testing in several settings. Therefore, a number of concepts in the primer are viewed or presented from various perspectives in the different chapters.

Second, one will also perceive some overlap between this primer and the critical pedagogy primer produced in this same series by Joe Kincheloe, a pedagogical thinker of the first order. This overlap reflects and highlights the necessary connections between pedagogy and critical pedagogy, neither one of which can stand without the other and, in the best of circumstances, are inextricably intertwined.

One must have models of good teaching to inspire, engage, and measure against. My teachers who themselves are great teachers have included Michael Apple, Herbert Kliebard, Todd Bender, and Frank Farley, to name just a few who profoundly reorganized my cognitive schema. I have also taught inspiring students at Queens College and the Graduate Center of the City University of New York who also taught me how to teach. As for colleagues, in addition to Joe Kincheloe, I have had the privilege of working with and learning from Greg Rubano, John Walsh, and the great scholar-teacher, Judith Summerfield.

CHAPTER ONE

The Problem of Pedagogy: The Cultural Contexts of Teaching

Teaching is the most complex of the professions in that it requires constant negotiation and attempted reconciliation of competing **worldviews**. Each pedagogical act reflects a dozen technical choices, all within a myriad of academic, cultural, and political questions. Further, none of those questions or answers is static or stable. Some elements of pedagogy may vary considerably simply in enacting disciplinary or subject matter expectations. After all, the humanist and the scientist rarely agree (Pepper, 1970).

Worldview
A term that indicates a comprehensive conception of the world, presented as an organic whole, from a particular point of view.

Teaching also responds to developmental demands. Third graders learn differently from high school seniors. And, within the larger multidisciplinary, multiage professional community, major differences in perceptions of the teacher's role and responsibilities regularly appear. Even the questions of whether education is a "discipline" and whether teachers need professional certification remain, unfortunately for our culture, open topics in some quarters (Finn, 2008; Klicka, 2007).

Ask any random group of citizens on the street about the responsibility of the teacher and most will say, "To keep the kids safe and under control and teach them the basics as cheaply as possible"; unless you ask them about *their* child's education and what they expect of their child's teachers. Many polls show that parents think most schools are in trouble, but not their child's school (Carroll, *Gallup Poll*, 2007). Moreover, most government officials today publicly demand that we hold teachers "accountable." "Getting tough" with teachers has become a route to political, if not necessarily educational, success. All of this attention has stirred up the professional debate as well, with volumes such as a recent collection by the National Society for the Study of Education, *Why Do We Educate? Renewing the Conversation*, appearing on a regular basis (Coulter & Wiens, 2008).

Despite these complications, teaching still requires complexity equal to the world we inhabit. One cannot teach in a simple way within a complex world and expect it to be anything other than an anachronistic political statement. In fact, teacher knowledge cannot be any simpler than the world in which it exists and still be useful as pedagogy. The teacher in the classroom is required to be the smartest one in the room. And, we are required to respect the value of children's developing knowledge and remain humble in our self-knowledge. Further, we are required to be students of our profession as well as teachers.

Pedagogy is the professional knowledge of the teacher, and the enacted practice of teaching, set within the context of theories of human development and learning, cultural reproduction and transformation, political and social progress, and intellectual engagement. In the end, the key questions about pedagogy remain centered on the:

- Nature of learning
- Sources of knowledge
- Role of the teacher

Although we know too much to pretend that the classroom is isolated from politics, we must also recognize that not every act of education is a political act. This last point is crucial because of the increasing partisanship of educational discourse, and the increasing use of schools as substitutes for actual social experiments in the larger society (Cheney, 1987).

"How do children learn?" is the central question of the modern era, an era defined educationally by the founding and the continuing sophistication of what is still called "child study" in many circles. Most of modern educational practice can be dated from the beginning of educational psychology—one of the new social sciences defining the great movement toward modern scientific research and scientific management in the Progressive Era. Scientific management, within the progressive movement, dominated U.S. scholarship and policy for the entirety of the 20th century. Science has brought many benefits to society, including improved health for most and, materially relevant to teachers, a culturally significant reduction in infant mortality. Under social science, the ideology and history of human culture are put to the test of naturalism and materialism, and beliefs and traditions are put to an empirical and experimental test (Callahan, 1962; Cremin, 1964; Hoftstadter, 1955).

The second central question, in its modern version, "What knowledge is of the most worth?" has been fought over continually, sometimes violently, as in the school bombings during the West Virginia textbook controversy in the 1970s (see Wikipedia on Kanawha County textbook controversy). Indeed, we are currently engaged in a "culture war" over school materials played out in newspaper editorials and within state school boards. These epistemological questions—questions about the nature of knowledge—could not be more unsettled in our times (for the neoconservative intellectual challenge, see, Cheney, 1989; Hirsch, 1988; Ravitch & Finn, 1988 A. Bloom, 1987;).

Creationism
An attempt to provide scientific proof for the origins of humans that coincides with the account in the Bible's Book of Genesis.

This epistemological argument starts at the metaphysical, or ontological, level: **creationism** versus *evolutionary theory* was recently at the center of a serious political debate when the Kansas State Board of Education attempted to require the teaching of creationism along with evolutionary history. Jurgen Habermas, the great contemporary philosopher of sociology of knowledge, argued recently that this ontological debate is a defining moment in the history of Western culture (2008). And so, like medieval theologians debating protestant scholars, modern classroom teachers find themselves at the center of the great philosophical debates of their time.

As for the third central question, contemporary visions of the teacher's role range from *in loco parentis* (in the place of a parent) on one end of the spectrum, to that of scripted factory worker (short-term, unskilled, and tightly controlled communicator of specific information) on the other. Teachers serve cultural roles, but not all members of the community agree on that role. The idea of *in loco parentis* is not something conservative, "family values" parents subscribe to willingly, and their definition of the teacher's role is frequently limited to the academic essentials. And, while more liberal, community-minded parents may desire their schools to teach "values," they want those values to be their own values. Teachers who violate community standards, even in divided communities, frequently find themselves under attack or even dismissed.

Pedagogy and Professionalism

In complex societies, teaching is a professional pursuit: it requires special knowledge, a period of apprenticeship, organized professional oversight, and certification by state authorities (as in other professions). Given the complexity and breadth of teaching and its knowledge base (pedagogy), one could say that writing a pedagogical **primer** is somewhat akin to figure skating on an ice cube. On the other hand, the topic of pedagogy is so large that one cannot even enter the discussion without a structured overview of the scope of issues and the nature of the questions. That is what this primer, like all primers, attempts: to provide some structure to begin to understand the range and the depth of the investigatory efforts required.

Primer
A short introduction to a subject, or a short book designed to teach children to read.

A primer also provides a **heuristic** for understanding a complex topic, and heuristics are at the heart of good teaching. Heuristics enable an understanding of cultural practices that can never be fully or completely understood because of their complexity. Whatever the cultural practice, a heuristic approach attempts to identify a set of epistemological assumptions and organize a culturally determined and culturally determining structure. Heuristics also protect against reducing a problem to something simpler, or merely analogical, so that a "definitive" answer can be asserted.

Heuristic
An exploratory or experimental problem-solving approach to understanding a concept or system.

For example, if teaching is reduced to the simple transfer of knowledge from an adult to a child, then a simple test of the child's knowledge after "teaching" has occurred would tell us how successful the teacher was at teaching. All study of teaching then could focus on assisting students in attaining better test scores. But, teaching is much more complex than simple transmission of information, and pedagogical practices require more than

Reify
To treat an abstraction as if it were a material or real thing.

High stakes testing
Basing school promotion and other real world decisions on a single standardized test score.

Operational definition
Defining something by its actions, rather than by its characteristics or traits.

telling the students what you know. And tests of knowledge are situated performances, even when we dignify and **reify** them as "**high stakes**." Simplification serves no role in pursuing complex purposes.

Pedagogy, while formally defining the teacher's professional knowledge, additionally represents the enactment of pedagogical thinking. This knowledge-in-action definition is sometimes called the **operational definition** of teaching. Operational definitions describe how something is performed, that is, what it looks like. However, these definitions describe behavior regardless of the intentionality of the person. For example, one could argue that teaching is taking attendance, or one could say that teaching is talking and admonishing and responding to students, all based on observing a classroom. In these sorts of observations, the "realistic" or "behaviorist" assumption is that intentions do not matter, but only the observed actions and the results do. Yet, what is observed is always determined by the stance and the expertise of the observer.

In professional pedagogical discourses, operational definitions tend to be presented either as "methods" of teaching or, in a more results-oriented manner, as "what works." The long history of teaching includes many "tricks of the trade." Some of those tricks of the trade are backed by study and research and focus on student learning. Some tricks of the trade continue because schools remain formal and bureaucratic, and these classroom strategies represent ways to control student behavior and manage the demands of the school as an institution. Therefore, sorting out an operational definition of teaching also requires setting expectations for teacher behavior—that is, operationally defining the teacher's role.

Almost all social science research, especially psychology, is based on operational definitions—descriptions of various behavioral and cognitive processes that stand in for the larger concept we cannot define comprehensively or formally. For example, one thing all good teachers ask when presented with findings of research that purport to improve the teaching of reading is: how is the experimenter defining *reading*? Many studies of "reading" actually investigate study skills or vocabulary or the ability to answer questions presented orally. Other studies that purport to study reading in general study only analytical reading. "What is the main idea of this story?" the researcher asks, though the "main idea" is something totally besides the point of reading fiction (Anderson & Rubano, 1991).

Given the performance requirements of teaching, pedagogical knowledge must be refined and realized through apprenticeship and professional practice. Formal professional development is enriched and transformed through experience. Oddly, some teachers who teach their students almost exclusively through **formal knowledge** recitation will tell you they learned nothing about teaching except through **experience**. Not coincidentally, there are some experienced professionals who are not very good at what they do, even though they continue to "teach" year after year with the same lessons and materials. They do not appear to "learn by doing" exclusively, though they must regularly pass some sort of minimum institutional standard for continued employment.

Formal knowledge
Knowledge that is rationalized, organized, and codified and frequently outside of one's everyday experience.

Experience
Direct observation or participation in events as a source of knowledge.

Further, teachers, like other professionals, are performing a social role while enacting cultural expectations. Approximately 90 percent of them are in a public school, an institution shaped by a set of government regulations and cultural imperatives developed over the past 150 years. Multiple generations of citizens have now experienced mass public schooling in the United States and carry their own expectations based on that experience. We never tire of saying how schooling was when *we* were kids, but who actually believes that schooling in the 1950s or 1960s, or in the 1990s for that matter, was anything like what schools and children are enduring today?

Parents express expectations for their children's passage through the public school system, followed by expected reward structures emanating from that system. In other words, parents expect their kids to get good jobs as a result of schooling, in addition to an education for citizenry and social melioration. State-supported school systems exist to promote the interests of the citizenry and the body politic. Teachers themselves frequently have expectations of schools based on their own student experiences—public school teachers who attended private or religious schools themselves have further complicated expectations.

And, last but not least, there are various political and cultural movements in this country seeking a return to a simpler time that accuse teachers of overstepping the grand traditions of schooling in America. Many of these conservatives appear to prefer home schooling, religious schooling, or private schooling. Unfortunately, there seems to be a highly disproportionate number of these folks, people with no personal experience of public education, in elected office and in governmental positions at any given time. However, many of the elite in our country continue to take full advantage of the public school system, which is still differentially financed primarily through local property tax assessments. The quality of the schools in a neighborhood continues to have a direct impact on housing values as well as on the educational opportunity for the children in the neighborhood.

Moreover, some educational policies are developed to meet political agendas predicated on limitation and exclusion. It took a Supreme Court decision ninety years after the Emancipation Proclamation to legally desegregate schools. Further, not all teachers are "liberals," as any school professional already knows, and discrimination of all sorts takes place within classrooms. Class, race, and gender considerations also undergird professional pedagogical expectations, both progressive and oppressive, mostly reflecting the "good intentions" of the teacher no matter how harmful these are in the larger scheme of things. Oppression frequently is excused with the assertion that we need to be "realistic" in working with some school populations.

Indeed, there appears to be a correlation between socioeconomic status (SES) and school achievement: poor students tend to do worse in school as a group than wealthier students. Therefore, there must also be a correlation between teacher pay and student achievement since wealthier districts pay higher salaries. Even the demographics of schooling are strangely skewed: the vast majority (approximately 80 percent) of teachers are non-Hispanic whites, and, at a minimum, 70 percent are women; socioeconomically, teachers are mostly middle class or emerging middle class (NCES, 2005). On the student side, at least half of the population is male, a large proportion is non-Caucasian, and a significant percentage low SES, among other demographic distinctions.

So, one wonders, how could questions about pedagogy be any more unsettled? And yet, as we shall see, the emphasis within pedagogy may fluctuate, but not the central structures and narratives. Pedagogies may differ depending on the setting and the context, but there are commonalities to teaching in all situations. The larger goals of pedagogy may formally change (we now assume that all citizens should complete high school, for example) but that does not affect the assumed possibilities for instruction. Pedagogy, ideally, is about opportunity and growth. According to recent opinion polls, most practitioners of democratic schooling also believe it is about equality of opportunity, if not outcome. In the end, teaching in the United States is about the community's responsibility to realize human potential and promote the democratic ideal, and a professional teacher is expected to offer no less in performance.

Pedagogical Confusion and Anti-pedagogy

Given the complexity of teaching, it seems strange that six-week boot camps for training aspiring teachers seem to have become the norm. Today, most big city superintendents promote quick-fix preparation programs glorifying on-the-job training, encapsulating pedagogy in a scripted lesson format. These policies beg the question of the purpose of pedagogy within these new knowledge factories, defined and driven as they are by high-stakes, external testing.

In this brave new world of schooling, pedagogical dialogues appear reduced to union rules and publicly reported test scores. Teachers are reduced to transient workers, most of whom stay no more than three years in the classroom. Alternate-route teacher preparation programs, though the definition of alternate is widely varying and in some places not so "alternative," are the preferred alternative to professionalism for many young people who have little interest in teaching as a career. Neoconservatives are actually arguing that teaching should be a short-term "gap year" exercise for post-baccalaureate students before pursuing graduate school or professional school (Finn, 2008).

Conservative/Liberal

Conservatism is a political position dedicated to the preservation of the status quo, or the existing situation. Liberalism is a political position promoting social progress and individual autonomy.

Traditional **conservative** liberal arts and sciences teaching practices are being rejected in favor of a neoconservative, business-driven, competitive approach to information transfer and job skill mastery. **Liberal** policies are dismissed, but most non-government, neoliberal reports on 21st-century learning demand a new media approach to education, envisioning an individualized machine-learning environment, as well as distance learning predicated on "asynchronous" study. This is not so far from the corporate approach. Politically, there are those who react against both neoliberal and neoconservative tendencies, focusing primarily on the political position associated with "social justice" and ignoring pedagogy as inadequate to their goal of transforming the larger society through school reorganization.

Within government policy, the No Child Left Behind Act (formerly Title I of the Elementary and Secondary Education Act) requires testing only in reading and mathematics, making pedagogy seem extravagant and a bit out of touch with the decisive, mechanistic, essentialist, and efficient times in which we now live. Moreover, given that the U.S. Department of Education Institute for Educational Sciences claims to possess scientific studies showing *exactly* how kids learn reading and mathematics, pedagogy has been tagged as a Romantic notion or as a remnant of the Aquarian Revolution of the 1960s. Pedagogy, focused as it is on *teacher* knowledge, is of little interest to those afraid or uncertain of teachers' influence in the classroom, or to those trying to replace teachers with machines or other cybernetic substitutes (Wiener, 1967).

Certainly, these are anti-pedagogical times. Schools, teachers, and educational practice have been under constant, withering attack since 1983's *A Nation at Risk*, the report of the Reagan-era commission that accused school professionals of *treason*: "If an unfriendly foreign power had attempted to impose on America the mediocre educational performance that exists today, we might well have viewed it as an act of war" (National Commission in Excellence, 1983, p. 1). In addition to the hallmarks of the Progressive Era that dominated thinking in most of the 20th century, most of the revolutionary transformation of schooling in the 1960s has been rejected. Ironically, and confusingly, some of the 1960s' best ideas and practices, such as the process model of writing, have been co-opted by the anti-pedagogical movement.

The anti-teacher, anti-pedagogy forces are embodied in both neoconservative policies and radical Left formulations that have resulted in everything from the end of the comprehensive high school to the entrance of the federal government, for the first time in history, into the local affairs of states and municipalities in the matter of schooling. In their visions of new schools, both conservative and radical minimize the role and function of teachers. Teachers are reduced to functionaries who are easily replaced and are generally interchangeable. That could explain why teacher preparation and pedagogical study are given short shrift by government policymakers and foundations headed by information industry billionaires.

While the New Right has commanded the most headlines and triumphed politically, the radical Left names teachers as dupes of the system (or even co-conspirators) or claims that teachers will never have any influence until the establishment of the Marxist utopian society fated, according to them, to replace capitalist oppression. On either end of this spectrum of determinism, professional teachers, formerly the center and the heart of the school, are reduced to either mechanistic pawns of politics or captives of ideology. As with all deterministic visions, these ignore the long history of individuals who have been transformative in our culture, and who normally thank their teachers in their award acceptance and inaugural speeches.

Most unfortunately, what has been lost in this battle of political wills is not simply humanistic reforms. Most of the post-*Sputnik* reforms in science and mathematics established in the name of national defense, originally funded under the 1958 National Defense Education Act, have also been abandoned in favor of basic skills. Foreign language instruction, normally part of most national defense curricula in the past, is practically non-existent. Not only has the baby been thrown out with the bath water, the bathtub has been set out on the curb. It is as if there was no history of teaching or schooling, except for some mythical little red schoolhouse. In fact, almost comically, images of the little red schoolhouse currently frame the entrance doors of the U.S. Department of Education building in Washington DC, like some postmodern **Potemkin village** plopped right in the middle of our nation's power center.

Potemkin village
A false, but impressive, façade put over or in front of something not so impressive on its own terms.

Even the time given to the traditional liberal arts, for long a conservative hallmark in curriculum reform, has evaporated: art, music, speech, and drama are missing from the required curriculum. The poorer the school, the more likely the loss; though even in the richest schools, parents are asked to pay for these "extracurricular" lessons and activities. Far from educating the whole child, some schools have now done away with physical education classes, even recesses, using these instead for test preparation. Social Studies in many curriculum proposals is limited to history. The cultural and aesthetic elements of English, the larger humanist perspectives, have been reduced to "literacy," with a big emphasis on "nonfiction" (Rosenblatt, 1980).

Legislatively, current federal and state policies evoke a limited, basic skills curriculum taught by part-time or short-term nonprofessionals who have received little or no preparation to teach, and who themselves are increasingly subject to top-down management and standardized test-driven evaluation of their students and themselves. Add to this the increasingly overcrowded classrooms, legal restrictions and requirements, wage and benefit degradation (combined with attacks on teacher unions), and increasing pressures to reduce school costs; is it any wonder that pedagogy seems a Victorian luxury available only to the elite or the out-of-touch-with-reality crowd?

Probably adding to the chaos is the seemingly perennial inability of anyone to sort out the issues plaguing both teachers and pedagogy at any time in history. Teachers definitely receive mixed signals. The confusion also afflicts their fellow-sufferers: children as well as parents and other ordinary taxpayers. The confusion is not from some deliberate political attempt to sabotage teaching. Though some of the current culture war is aimed directly at teachers, teachers mostly suffer collateral damage.

For example, one primary attack of the neoconservative movement has been on public employee unions, including teachers' unions. If one looks closely at many of the proposed school "reforms," a significant number appear premised on a solution that requires doing away with collective bargaining. In fact, one of the central features of the charter school movement includes provisions that allow these taxpayer-funded public schools to hire nonunion, and uncertified, teachers.

Pedagogy per se is not merely a political stance, but the rights that unions guarantee are important to more than the "working conditions" argument. For example, woman teachers were paid less than men teachers until collective bargaining appeared; that fact alone makes collective bargaining a cultural as well as economic movement. Culturally, any school system that values professionals differently because of gender or race or class limits the definition and purpose of pedagogy in those classrooms.

However, while union contracts provide equity for teachers within a district, wealthier districts pay teachers more than the less affluent areas can afford. And, attempts to shift tax dollars away from wealthy suburbs to equalize funding for poor urban districts has cost several state governors their re-election over the past two decades. And, even within schools, there are widely varying resources for the different tracks of students, even when the tracks are not officially acknowledged.

On the other hand, wage equity—or even certification of teachers by the state, for that matter, or even equal funding under the law—does not necessarily promise better teaching by anyone. And for that matter, teachers in private and religious schools are exempt from most of those regulatory functions and still manage to teach generally successfully. These private school professionals are not allowed membership in the National Education Association, but they still manage to be organized professionally (**NAIS**, e.g.). One's institutional affiliation does not affect the quality of teaching, but only the possibilities for schooling. Being a good teacher means different things in different settings, but being in a "good" setting does not automatically make one a "good" teacher.

NAIS/NCTE/NCTM/ MENC, etc.
Acronyms of the names of professional educators' organizations in various disciplines or interest groups.

Opportunities for professional definition and development exist within the various subject matter disciplines such as the National Council of Teachers of Mathematics and other parallel organizations (MENC, NCTE, etc.). Public, private, and religious schoolteachers, working together, have organized themselves around their mutual pedagogical concerns in these organizations; membership in these groups is one way to remain connected professionally in the increasingly isolated classroom. In a sign of the times, these subject matter organizations are mainly headquartered in the surrounds of Washington DC, with most retaining professional lobbyists on the payroll. The political element of teaching cannot be ignored in an attempt to be a "purist," because, regardless of all this organizing around the topic of pedagogy, we always need to ask ourselves: for what and for whom are we accomplishing all this better teaching and better learning? Who benefits from the actions of teachers in the nation's classrooms (Habermas, *Knowledge and Human Interests*, 1970)?

Teaching and Learning in School

One other fundamental issue that confuses the discussion of pedagogy lies in the distinctions between *teaching* and *schooling*. Schools promote a social and political purpose to which teachers contribute regardless of their intentions. If a teacher does not "control" a classroom, the teacher is removed as "incompetent." But schooling inhabits a larger institutional and social sphere than pedagogy. Pedagogy is primarily about *teaching* content and skills (to use one formulation), and not about college counseling or supervising the prom or teaching kindergarten kids to stand in a line.

Teachers do fulfill various institutional roles: they counsel, they control behavior, they promote general social and cultural development, all of which serves the kids and society in a variety of ways (providing a safe and productive environment, for example). Pedagogy itself always assumes a humanist stance and always functions in a human context, so teachers are always teaching social norms and culturally expected behavior even as they teach academic knowledge or structure learning experiences.

There also is the constant confusion regarding the realms of teaching and the scientific conduct of research on learning. Most educational psychologists will claim that their research on learning has nothing to do with teaching. They insist that it is "up to the teacher to figure out how to apply the research findings." This split between teaching and learning shows up even in the language of representation, in which the pedagogical disciplinary field is styled "curriculum and teaching" or "curriculum and instruction" depending on the strength of the educational psychology influence at the particular institution of higher learning. The point, for the moment, is that learning theory is almost never based on assumptions of formal learning in classroom settings, and when it is, the teacher is frequently categorized in studies on student learning as an unwanted, additional "**uncontrolled variable**."

Uncontrolled variable
Researchers attempt to control variables so that the only uncontrolled variable is the one they are trying to measure. In educational psychology, the uncontrolled variable is usually the learning task performed by the learner.

Recently, these competing notions of teaching and learning have been mysteriously recast within assessment circles, especially those frequented by educational psychologists of a mechanistic sort and many policymakers. In those discussions, reports, and policy documents, the title "curriculum and *teaching*" has been changed to "curriculum and *assessment*." In other words, in this formulation, the active agent—the teacher and the attendant *teaching*—is no longer in the equation for student and school success. In this "curriculum and assessment" representation, apparently all that is needed is to specify the curriculum and assess the student learning. In between the two steps, of course, is where most of the knowledge of pedagogy and the work of teaching exist.

Behaviorist
A psychological school that assumes that the only objective evidence that can be studied is one's actions, usually characterized as stimulus and response measures.

But, even the strictly **behaviorist** educational psychologists, the ones who want students to use programmed, sequenced, individualized learning systems that do not require a "teacher," recognize a pedagogy implicit in their learning systems and machines. The problem with that "pedagogy" is that it can be rationalized for machine learning (especially in artificial intelligence models) and for training animals, but it rarely meets the more sophisticated requirements of educating human beings (Wiener, 1967). To be fair, a new breed of psychological researchers in recent years have gone out of their way to attach social and even cultural variables to their research designs (Cole, 1996; Cole & Scribner, 1974). But the dominant view remains that of the behaviorist looking for the elusive "intelligent tutor" program to control the act of teaching and to determine the learning.

However, conservative humanist intellectuals of various stripes have driven the anti-pedagogical bandwagon throughout most of the 20th century, the most influential being Irving Babbitt in the 1920s and Mortimer Adler from the 1930s through the 1980s. Diane Ravitch, Lynne Cheney, Chester Finn, Allan Bloom, and E. D. Hirsch, Jr. have been the most influential since 1984. The past twenty-five years, since *A Nation at Risk*, represent one long, sustained attack on professional teaching and pedagogical study.

I am reminded of something I heard asserted by someone who was minimizing the value of teacher preparation and certification: all anyone needs to teach is knowledge of the discipline, good character, and the ability to communicate the disciplinary knowledge to the students. First, this assertion ignores the small obstacle that each of those criteria is impossible to define precisely. Secondly, it fails to acknowledge that none of the three assertions is simple or uncontested. The above statement reduces all pedagogy, the actual teaching part, to "communicate knowledge to the students."

One could suppose that the above simplified formula represents something equivalent to teaching someone to drive by telling them how to do it, or teaching someone to read by being a good person and a good reader oneself, or teaching a child U.S. history by just telling her everything you know about U.S. history that you learned in college (and from 20 to 40 years of living). What could be simpler, especially if you already possess the good character that guarantees that you will not harbor any doubts about what you are doing?

Consequently, given your good character and your intrinsic interest and expertise in U.S. history, what could possibly keep your 30+ students in your overcrowded classroom from "learning" the knowledge you have communicated (other than their defective character or simple laziness, as some columnists and legislators argue)? This stance embodies part of a recent attempt to simplify culture and cultural practices in the name of control. If one accepts this simple, exclusionary definition, then one does not need to grapple with all the other issues that one may not agree with politically or culturally. For example, if there is no "race problem," no one needs to fix it. If learning English is simply about nationalism, social immersion, and personal commitment, no one needs to worry about bilingualism. If a child's "behavior problem" is merely biological or physiological, it is easy to simply prescribe drugs to solve the problem.

Finally, we as teachers need to acknowledge and address the American tradition of commonsense and "can do" pragmatism. Many Americans are proudly anti-intellectual, a tradition that extends back to Puritan times and is maintained today through an insistence on the superiority of "commonsense" over "egghead" thinking (Hofstadter, 1966). We believe in action over words and still respect the strong silent type who can, as President Bush declared, be "The Decider." Several of our most recent presidents, most holding a degree or two from Harvard and Yale, have affected a "cowboy" or "good ole boy" public persona. The phenomenon has a long history; after Andrew Jackson's 1828 victory representing the ascendance of U.S. frontier or Western interests, most 19th-century presidential candidates claimed to be born in a log cabin. Certainly, there are times when everyone becomes tired of the seemingly endless abstraction in Western intellectual circles, and the general disparagement of committee work by professionals reflects our impatience with mere "talk." But, commonsense, the prized American "character trait," is no more than a calculated social construct meant to reduce dialogue and limit the discussion.

Admittedly, it is from experience that we learn much of what we know (and can do). Besides, much of the recent distrust of "theory" stems from a seeming lack of any practical exhibition of any particular theory's application to life. In pedagogy, these theoretical formulations, without attachment to classroom practice, simply widen the gap between theory and practice. Conversely, however valuable experience might be, most of the great accomplishments of the 20th century involved projects for which experience simply was not available, from space travel (astrophysics) to the Internet (communications theory) to plastics (modern chemistry) to genetics (molecular biology). Note also that none of these were available by simply applying commonsense.

Organized, complicated societies usually require specialized cultural practices possible only through formal teaching, so teachers certainly serve a necessary role in complex societies. The administrative form in which the teaching takes place is almost irrelevant to the task, because the teacher's role transcends social and political and, certainly, architectural limitations. Even the overheated or un-air-conditioned classroom cannot stop teaching and learning from happening, however uncomfortably. And, specialized roles normally require specialized knowledge: teachers are defined by the notion of pedagogy, the specialized knowledge of the professional educator. Without pedagogical knowledge, any one residing in a school building is simply part of the support services or, worse, part of the furniture.

However good we are at teaching, there are always other cultural and social forces working against our best intentions. Not all teaching is automatically successful: teaching and teachers may have a variable effect even in the best of circumstances for formal education, or even with the knowledge of "best practices." Luigi Cavalli-Sforza, the originator of the deep DNA project that has now mapped out the major migrations of humans in prehistory and a geneticist imbued with a lifetime of research on human evolution, writes in *Genes, Peoples, and Languages*:

> Most cultural characteristics are transmitted by a variety of means that often conflict. This conflict is common; for instance, it occurs when one learns rules of behavior at school that differ from those taught at home.... The consequences of these conflicts vary significantly among individuals and particular cultural traits.
>
> Cultural transmission comprises education received from both family and school. It also includes all the habits and customs that are not explicitly part of one's education. Certainly, an individual acquires these through personal experience, but here again, conscious or unconscious imitation must play an important part. (2000, p. 187)

Amongst other important points made by Cavalli-Sforza above is the recognition of the role of the unconscious in learning. Not all of our knowledge figures as part of our conscious understanding. Some knowledge is "tacit," or, as the saying goes, sometimes we "know more than we can say" (Polanyi, 1962). In other words, even what we do know may not be obvious to us; we may not be able to explain how we did something or even explain what we mean when we say something. Most people cannot explain how they ride a bicycle; most cannot formally define important words they use on a regular basis, ranging from "wow" to "critical" to "assessment" to "love."

Many expert teachers cannot teach formally how they get the class to "settle down" or explain the ways in which they modify their voice or facial expression to communicate both behavioral and academic cues. In fact, they may not be even aware they are doing it. Many teachers cannot explain how they write, and no one in the history of scientific research has been able to accurately describe the process of reading, even operationally, let alone define it formally. So much for the U.S. Department of Education's claims that they know scientifically how children learn to read; they must be using a limited, operational definition of only a specified and limited type of reading activity.

Automaticity
Doing something well enough that one does not consciously think about how it is done.

However, although one of the hallmarks of any professional is **automaticity**, that is, the practice that emanates from tacit expert knowledge, the central core of professional behavior encompasses the continuing effort to understand and articulate one's own practice. Even if we restricted ourselves to the professional knowledge of the teacher and the tradition of teacher practice, we would still find myriad conflicts within our professional culture regarding the role, the knowledge base, and the function of the teacher. Some of those conflicts are historical, some are cultural, some administrative, and so on. We can pretend that nothing exists outside of our classroom or we can act as professionals within a larger community of practice (Wenger, 1999).

To complicate things further, every academic discipline embraces conflicts about it own nature, sometimes reshaping the borders of the discipline on a regular basis. Within the school subject of Social Studies, for example, some insist that teachers and texts focus on history and demand that all teachers should be history teachers. Other scholars and policymakers insist on social science training and a knowledge base of sociology, anthropology, and political science for teachers. Most state education authorities try to construct some sort of compromise between the two positions, usually requiring both competing paradigms, with varying degrees of success.

Moreover, knowledge of the discipline each of us teaches is rife with controversies and competing theories, as well as distortions, mysteries, speculations, and even some scholarly bullying. The more serious the scholar, the more likely that she will promote new approaches to the field, in the process attempting to demonstrate the inadequacy of the current dominant approach. Most scholars pursuing studies are looking for knowledge they do *not* know. A teacher-scholar is someone who introduces students to the controversies within a field of thought, rather than just communicate simple "information." *Certainty* is a trademark of only those who do not know something very deeply or do not embrace the scholarly notion of skepticism.

Finally, everyone who teaches, formally or informally, does so on the basis of cultural assumptions. Pedagogy is a means to formally and intellectually address those fundamental questions, rather than leaving them to tacit knowledge. Just experiencing teaching will not make you a better teacher. Even if you are a good "intuitive" teacher, without articulation and reflection you cannot grow. This is true even if you believe you have the "gift" of teaching, as if any one single nebulous factor can explain anything. And experience has its limits as Mark Twain reminds us with characteristic wit and wisdom:

> We should be careful to get out of an experience only the wisdom that is in it—and stop there; lest we be like the cat that sits down on a hot stove lid. She will never sit down on a hot stove lid again—and that is well; but also she will never sit down on a cold one anymore. (1897, "Pudd'nhead Wilson's New Calendar," headnote to *Following the Equator,* Chapter IX)

Twain was a great teacher himself because of that combination of wit and wisdom; all teachers could use such a combination to make learning more powerful.

Without knowledge and reflection one remains static in a changing world. In that case, teachers can remain only as good as they currently are, while simultaneously becoming increasingly irrelevant. Better professional practice is also about articulating what one is doing "right" as well as what one may be doing "wrong."

This dictum applies to responsibility to the profession as well: teachers have a responsibility not only to the students they teach but also to other teachers who follow in the next generations.

Cultural Practices and Teaching

We cannot directly change the political, social, and economic issues that drive much of schooling and limit teachers' roles and range of influence. Significantly, most of the larger meritocratic expectations for schooling are dominated by private testing corporations such as Educational Testing Service (ETS) and American College Testing (ACT), overseen by nonprofit, nongovernment groups such as the College Board. Most citizens, including teachers, cannot answer questions such as "Who put the College Board, a nonprofit group headquartered near Lincoln Center in Manhattan, in charge of assessing public school students throughout the US?"

The College Board's Advanced Placement (AP) courses set the standard for both school and college curriculum, with passing scores being cashed in for college credit at state universities and private colleges alike. How could AP courses serve both purposes and simultaneously receive both college credit *and* high school credit? Teachers in schools teach those AP courses, but the curriculum is fixed and tested by college professors and College Board/ETS employees. Here is a business, sanctified by its nonprofit status, in the heart of our national curriculum, a business entity defining public education policy.

These standardized tests define knowledge and dictate pedagogy through their content-based testing models. And these tests have come to define high-stakes testing, even though their very nature (i.e., mass, norm-referenced testing) means the material will be standardized and limited in scope. And given the social efficiency rationales used by states for employing these companies, one would be hard pressed not to mention the increasing problems these companies are having in providing accurate or timely results from these high-stakes tests. Recently, ETS was fired by the British government for continuing mistakes in administering and reporting on the UK national school tests, tests that are truly high stakes (Mansell, 2008).

Those hegemonic conditions, what the neoconservatives have termed the public school "monopoly," along with the relative absence of men and persons of color from the teaching population, do not present ideal conditions for comprehensive and representative education within the culture. Within our culture, the "solutions" put forth to "solve" these problems are many and varied. Some of the solutions are ideological, some are financial, some are pragmatic, and some are bureaucratic. But in the end, pedagogy is necessary to the development of the individual as a teaching professional, because, in the end, teaching is about *personal* responsibility to the students, the community, and the future.

How does one resolve one's vision of oneself as a teacher with various competing notions of pedagogy; how does one remain individuated while still serving the community? Pedagogy encompasses serious political, social, and cultural domains that enact and sometimes fight against the wishes of the common culture. Some teachers regard themselves as dissenting from the perceived popular culture, while others envision themselves undermining the official culture of the school. State-supported schools, by definition, are designed to provide official cultural knowledge and seem equally intended to warn about or even work against popular culture. These scenarios are at the heart of the debate over the progressives' "reconstruct society" ideology versus the conservatives' "preserve the status quo" functions of schooling ideologies. Of course, those two positions ignore the stances of the radical Left and the radical Right, both of which promote a destruction of the current system, but few people who feel that strongly about the current system of education are attracted to teaching as the transformative strategy.

In any case, much of popular culture is deliberately excluded from teaching in a formal setting. For example, it is rare to find a school-sponsored rock band. On the other hand, many teachers see themselves as subverting official culture in their teaching, providing examples and ideas from the popular media or promoting alternative ways of addressing knowledge and building skills. The point here is that there is a tension between the "official culture," represented by textbooks and materials, school administration and state-mandated curriculum, and the popular culture represented by the world outside of school.

These days, popular culture provides an increasingly sophisticated alternative to the standard school curriculum. Some would say popular culture provides a material and obvious critique of current schooling and would argue that the current school curriculum is completely out of touch with 21st-century culture. James Gee and many of the New Literacy advocates argue that even the brand of literacy we provide, mostly text-based, offers little to students who are immersed in multimedia culture (2004). Strangely, the movement in school policy in recent years has been toward not only a more limited and controlled curriculum, but to an even more text-based assessment based almost exclusively on reading (Willinsky, 1990).

Some would argue that this limited curriculum, along with its equally limited tests, is a result of a conservative political reaction against alleged "liberal" changes in the culture. The current curriculum situation, especially the testing, is merely a case of using schools to return children to old-fashioned values. Other critics, notably from the Marxist school, argue that the schools are deliberately designed to provide only a tightly controlled basic curriculum. Both neoliberal and neoconservative elites, the political Left argues, do not want to provide meaningful educations for coming generations of citizens who will serve only as minimum wage service workers (Aronowitz, 2004; Willis, 1981). Whatever the reasoning, current expectations for teaching the official curriculum appear to be teaching more simply and teaching less, while the culture becomes richer and more complex.

Though pedagogy is historical and individuated, cultural hegemony always influences what is considered "good" teaching. Schools exist to further the culture in which they exist, so schools carry with them assumptions, developed over generations, about the function of schools in their particular culture. Having argued that the teacher possesses professional knowledge and purpose, and that the curriculum ultimately resides in the individual teacher, there is a need to show how society, culture, institutions, and professional communities define or at least constrain the teacher (Schubert, 1986). The following are part of the history of teaching and, therefore, part of expectations in every teacher's classroom.

Systematic formal schooling begins in the U.S. with the Massachusetts Bay Colony's "Old Deluder Law" of 1647, when the colonists determined that it was the responsibility of the community to teach children to read and write so that their ignorance of the Bible and other good books would not make them fall prey to Satan, the "Old Deluder" (Krug, 1966). Here is a moral rationale with practical consequences, including a law describing the ways of assessing taxes for purposes of hiring a teacher. The teacher held a very specific purpose in Puritan society, as did all things in Puritan society that were seen as dictated by God, the source of all authority. From then until now, as the United States has grown and diversified and morphed into an imperial power, there has been a continuing and evolving discussion about the role of the teacher in society.

Whereas many other world cultures treat teachers as objects of veneration with a somewhat exalted status, America's archetypal teacher is Ichabod Crane, the scrawny, cowardly protagonist of "The Legend of Sleepy Hollow," Washington Irving's short story classic. A long catalog of Ichabod's physical shortcomings is summarized by the image of "some scarecrow eloped from a cornfield," and he is further characterized as having a "soft and foolish heart" (1819/1983, pp. 1061, 1066). When teachers are not portrayed as feminized males in American culture, they are usually portrayed as caring men who "get tough" with juvenile delinquents. American films run the entire gamut from *The Blackboard Jungle* (Brooks, 1955) to *Lean on Me* (Avildsen, 1989). Women teachers are frequently portrayed as victims, such as Sandy Dennis's character in *Up the Down Staircase* (Mulligan, 1967), unless they are military veterans and are then interchangeable with caring tough men, such as Michelle Pfeiffer's ex-military character in *Dangerous Minds* (Smith, 1995). In these popular narratives of schooling, exceptional individuals who never intended to be teachers, working solely within school settings, but, paradoxically, working "outside the system", solve impossible educational problems. Sidney Poitier's character in *To Sir With Love*, though English in setting, is the ultimate modern teacher who sacrifices everything for the good of the students, the sacrifice symbolized by the stylized crucifixion pose he assumes at a key point in the film (Clavell, 1967).

Progressive
The use of scientific research, democratic processes, and innovative technologies to continuously evolve society.

In our time, of course, we are enmeshed in a "culture war," and teachers are somewhere on the battlefield, currently being *blitzkrieged* by superintendents, mayors, professors, columnists, governors, and presidents. On one hand is the liberal-**progressive** movement of the first eighty years of the 20th century, codified into law during the Franklin Delano Roosevelt presidency (The New Deal, 1932–1945) and further realized under the "Great Society" of Lyndon Johnson (1963–1968). On the other hand is a neoconservative reaction to that liberalism beginning with the election of Ronald Reagan in 1980 and continuing since, though there has been a powerful conservative reaction against progressive thinking throughout the 20th century.

In most of the current escalating warfare, educators are portrayed as liberals, and it would be fair to say that most teachers see themselves as educated and open-minded (though these days that might be called "independent" or "libertarian"). But, many surveys demonstrate that teachers are no different from the population at large, running the spectrum from radical Left to radical Right with most in the middle, politically and culturally, representing a mix of beliefs and ideologies. Anyone who has spent time in a teacher's workroom knows this is true.

As should be obvious from the range of social and cultural issues cited, we should be talking about *pedagogies,* rather than pedagogy. The grand tradition of pedagogy is the *humanistic,* with roots in the Renaissance (and a nod or two to the ancient Greeks). The humanistic tradition in modern times is benchmarked by the publication of Matthew Arnold's *Culture and Anarchy* in 1867 and is continued today by the advocates of "cultural literacy." In this humanistic tradition, schooling serves to civilize humans, so teachers are purveyors of social tradition and promoters of the cultural imperative. However, in an aggressively antisocial setting, in a society bent on oppressing its citizens, teachers and schools can serve those purposes as well. Humanism goes by many different guises and can be a liberator or an oppressor depending on one's particular position in society.

On the other hand, what most teaching and research professionals are referring to when they talk about pedagogy is the *scientific-technological* model, the liberal-progressive approach to schooling that began in the early 20th century with psychological studies and now encompasses all of the social sciences. Though most of modern schooling is driven by "science," what constitutes science differs among various groups. Science can be a vehicle of human potential, serving to undermine the feudal system of the Middle Ages and saving humans from any number of epidemics and disease. Science also produced the means of combat for the bloody warfare in the first half of the 20th century in which millions of innocent civilians died from advanced weaponry. In schools, science can be either a teacher of modern thinking, as in the scientific method, or a mostly male-dominated body of secret knowledge available only to the initiated.

There is also a third school of thought on pedagogy that some would call a *craft* model. Derogatorily, this version is represented as the "bag of tricks" or even the "personality" model. But the craft model references important oral traditions of teaching drawn from classroom experiences over many generations. Teachers' unions and school district-based teacher-preparation models emphasize the craft model. The craft model governs the day-to-day lives of teachers. Sometimes the craft model carries great wisdom and sometimes it prevents innovation.

Each of these approaches to pedagogy represents not merely technical differences, but different worldviews. Each approach brings its own ideology and subsequent expectations for teachers and students. In each of the cases above, there is no case of "either/or" or "black/white" or "hot/cold." In discussions of concepts, most people do not agree with one side or the other but fit somewhere along a continuum of thought. On the traditional "discipline and freedom" continuum, there are some people who are all discipline (totalitarian schooling) or all freedom (natural schooling), but most of us lie somewhere along the continuum in our thinking. Some of us lean more toward the discipline end of the spectrum and some toward the freedom side to varying degrees. And, that thinking might change based on situation and condition.

Hypothetical Positions in Teacher Thinking/Beliefs

General Thinking/Belief:
Freedom ----------------X---------------- Discipline
Friday Afternoon:
Freedom ---------X---------------------- Discipline
Test Preparation:
Freedom ----------------------------X---- Discipline

Teachers do not remain unchanged in every situation in our classrooms. Context and circumstances shape our thinking. We are not independent agents or context-free.

One other consideration is that teachers teach differently given different student populations. Urban school populations are different from their counterparts in the suburbs, with big differences in terms of teaching practices in their schools (Anderson & Summerfield, 2004). Students in the "remedial" tracks receive different treatment than students in the "honors" track. Oddly, while recent government policy promotes a common curriculum for all through **standardized testing** and denigrates vocational programs, universities are creating "honors colleges" to segregate the "best and brightest" from the rest of the students. These newly tracked populations are subject to different curricula, enhanced experiences, and special teaching (and even free computers and tuition, i.e., special *treatment*).

Standardized testing
A test designed to compare members of a group consistently and reliably.

Historically, the public high school became a "**comprehensive**" institution with the passing of the Smith-Hughes Act for Vocational Education in 1917. Federal money was supplied to hire teachers and provide resources for teaching agriculture, home economics, and trade and industrial subjects in addition to the liberal arts and sciences (Krug, 1966, p. 114). Thus began the idea that schools would be focused not just on college preparation in academic subjects but also on a range of educational activities meant to provide skilled employment and to improve society. Significantly, at least from the perspective of the current culture war, one of the key provisions of President Johnson's War on Poverty was the Vocational Education Act of 1963, which provided federal funding for high school curricula that covered almost all training "except those demanding professional training and college degrees" (Krug, 1966, p. 115).

Comprehensive schooling
Educating the whole child and providing education appropriate to a child's, as well as society's, needs.

One of the earliest acts of the Reagan administration in 1981 was to effectively eliminate federal funding for vocational education in public schools. The basic argument centered on the need to do away with "tracking" in schools, to oppose differentiated curricula in favor of a core curriculum, and to return schools to a focus on the basic academic subjects. The political motive, like much of neoconservative policy, was to undo federal government practices established either under the New Deal in the 1930s or the Great Society initiatives of the 1960s.

Certainly, schools had tried to become everything to everyone over the three decades since World War II. In the 1970s, the curriculum was mostly elective (in emulation of the college model), values clarification and various other counseling approaches had become dominant (mirroring talk therapy in the society at large), and vocational students were actively discriminated against, both academically and culturally (watch the "auto shop" segment of any school documentary from the 1960s or the 1970s). But, clearly, the neoconservative reformers did not do away with the notion of **leadership education**. "Leadership" has become the mantra of this new conservative era with every CEO's and ex-mayor's ghost-written biography shouting out "leader" or "prince" or some other clear indication of this current status marker.

Leadership education
School policy asserting that the "best and brightest" must be given special and separate education to enhance their future leadership positions in society.

Historically, the notion of the liberal arts (and sciences) as *leadership education*, as necessary for the *humanizing* of the elites, begins in the Renaissance with Sir Thomas Elyot's, *The Boke Named the Governour* [*sic*] (1531), a manual for educating princes who would be future rulers. Renaissance era rulers took great pride in their humanistic learning and used their educations to define humanistic government: England's King Henry VIII and his daughter Elizabeth I serve as examples. *The Boke Named the Gouvernor* joined other books describing the proper conduct of princes and kings, most notoriously Machiavelli's treatise on statesmanship, *The Prince* (1513). But Elyot's book was focused on teaching the young and grooming them for their roles, clearly a pedagogical treatise in its intent and execution. He introduced the word "maturity" (usurped it from Latin, he said) to describe the results of his pedagogical machinations, a word we still use to describe a person exhibiting desirable adult qualities.

Leadership education still exists as a core concept in American education, most obviously demonstrated in the titles of numerous new public and private schools labeled "Leadership Academies," including Oprah Winfrey's new school in South Africa. And, the liberal arts ideal remains part of the curriculum discussions in elite schools and universities, for the same reason that Thomas Elyot argued in the 16th century: future leaders need to rule wisely for the general good of the people. The teachers at schools for the elite take this charge very seriously: it becomes the rationale for imparting general education in the liberal arts and sciences against modern expert specializations promoted by the increasing complexity of the scientific and technical world. Most of our political leaders possess leadership credentials, most of them with degrees from elite schools, and have been socialized to the same notions of leadership and citizenry through these prerequisite leadership educations.

In the "good old days," the lower classes frequently received the most basic education, if they were not denied an education altogether. Illiteracy was the norm; in some cases, it was even illegal to educate oppressed populations, such as the enslaved populations in the U.S. before the Civil War. The liberal-progressive invention of the comprehensive high school and our current movement toward universal high school attendance, with a recurring goal of universal graduation, are twentieth-century phenomena. Recent neoconservative and neoliberal policies have tried to educate all students in the common school to the same set of cultural knowledge, values, and skills. The best possible outcome of those policies would be a liberalizing and humanistic education for all students.

What is certainly a further conundrum within the problematic nature of education discourse is that we allow, unlike the fields of law and medicine, those who do not believe in the intellectual paradigm to engage in the professional dialogue. Though supposedly one of the best-selling books of all time, *Doctor Atkins' New Diet Revolution* is rarely part of the professional dialogue in medicine or nutrition. These popular "weight loss" books, like other bestselling exposés in public health or social policy, blame a conspiracy as the source of the problem. In Atkins' case, he alleges a conspiracy between food companies and the American Medical Association. These conspiracy books inevitably provide a single answer to the problem, with an accusation that a conspiracy of interests of the powerful keeps the simple solution from being implemented. The medical profession rightly rejects these books from the professional discourse.

And yet, in education, we take these books and authors seriously. E. D. Hirsch, Jr.'s *Cultural Literacy* (1988), a highly influential book, is structurally the same as the diet books that crowd the top of the nonfiction bestseller list. *Cultural Literacy* provides a single solution to a complex problem and accuses the profession that oversees that area of inquiry of engaging in a conspiracy of "experts" to defraud the common citizen for selfish or misguided reasons. Hirsch blames liberal-progressive educators, along with teacher organizations and unions, for the "decline" in content knowledge in the U.S. Further, he asserts, the motive of conspiracy is a teacher unions' and teaching professionals' need to protect their "monopoly" on education research for their own mysterious goals. Hirsch cannot simply present his educational ideas; instead he needs to base his version of the "crisis" on a conspiracy of liberals lead by the Old Deluder himself (at least according to neoconservatives): John Dewey.

These popular diatribes do affect teachers when parents, administrators, and political operatives attack the local school curriculum. In some ways, this is a legal battle, not a pedagogical one, because it is always predicated on the rights of the parents or the students or the taxpayers. And, sometimes, that battle is predicated on the rights of the teachers. But the teacher already has most of the rights by virtue of her position. The best way to look at pedagogical concerns is by listing not the teacher's rights, but the teacher's professional responsibilities for teaching. The teacher should be concerned first and foremost with pedagogy and not fall prey to popular "commonsense" solutions as a substitute for professional behavior.

In the end, while the role of schooling is contained within the topic of pedagogy, the role of the teacher is defined by pedagogy. The definition of pedagogical thinking that we assert reflects the value we place on teachers and on teaching. And, certainly, how we define pedagogy has everything to do with how we think children should be educated and how adults should live in the world. Professional knowledge of teachers in democratic societies needs to reflect the potential of democratic thinking. A teacher still needs to teach so that the students can learn, but we are always situated in a power struggle. To not teach in a politically situated manner is to leave our students at the mercy of the their surroundings, as Dewey said,

> If [the student] has not powers of deliberation and invention, he must pick up his ideas casually and superficially from the suggestions of his environment and appropriate the notions which the interests of some class insinuate into his mind. (1908, p. 438)

Pedagogy requires serious attention in a democracy. Deliberation and invention, as well as both critical and creative thinking, are necessary to our participation in a free society. And teachers are a central source for learning those elemental ways of living.

Glossary

Automaticity—Doing something so well that one does not think consciously about how it is done. Assumes experience and repetition on the part of the learner as well as a holistic understanding of the process. Sometimes related to "tacit knowledge"—knowledge that you possess but cannot formally explain.

Behaviorist—A psychological school that assumes that the only objective evidence that can be studied is one's actions, usually characterized as stimulus and response measures. Both behaviorism and cognitivism are reductionist theories in their assumptions about humans, seeing human thought and behavior as reducible to discrete and identifiable components governed by discoverable rules.

Comprehensive schooling—The doctrine that school can serve all the needs of the population. Based on the notion of educating the whole child and providing appropriate education to a child's needs, comprehensive education includes traditional formal learning, vocational training, and physical (psychomotor) experiences. Though the current trend is toward "academic essentialism," many schools in economically disadvantaged neighborhoods provide medical care and other social services for students.

Conservative/Liberal—Conservatism is a political position dedicated to the preservation of the status quo, or the existing situation. Liberalism is a political position promoting social progress and individual autonomy. Modern neoconservatives promote democracy and American national culture and interests in international affairs. Neoliberals discard some traditional liberal concerns for a more pragmatic approach to social progress. All of the above are moderate positions and are not to be confused with extreme Rightist or Leftist positions, both of which tend to be antigovernment.

Creationism—A recent pseudoscientific doctrine meant to challenge evolutionary biology. Supporters attempt to provide "scientific proof" for the origins of humans that coincides with the account in the Bible's Book of Genesis.

Experience—Direct observation or participation in events as a source of knowledge. The most complicated word in educational discussion when used as a transitive verb. Experience is the most difficult word in human understanding, along with "being," when used as a noun.

Formal knowledge—Usually contrasted with experiential knowledge, formal knowledge tends to be rationalized, organized, and codified and frequently outside of one's everyday experience. For example, though everyone can speak comprehensibly in everyday discourse, it does not require knowledge of the formal rules of grammar. Formal knowledge is also contrasted with informal knowledge, an educational stance that promotes connections between school knowledge and commonsense knowledge.

Heuristic—An exploratory or experimental problem-solving approach to understanding a concept or system.

High stakes testing—Basing school promotion and other real world decisions on a single standardized test score. Semantically, it appears to be derived from the notion of high stakes poker playing. Currently the government's policy of choice, high stakes testing has been criticized by various fair testing groups, such as FairTest, and by many professional educators as limiting and discriminatory.

Leadership education—The belief that some individuals, "the best and the brigh*test,*" are intrinsically superior to others and are "natural" leaders. A school policy that asserts that those individuals must be given special and separate education to build their future leadership positions in society. A variation on the idea of *noblesse oblige*, the traditional notion that responsible behavior is expected of those of high rank. In the U.S., especially among graduates of elite colleges, the *noblesse oblige* rationale is also constituted as "giving something back" to society.

NAIS/NCTE/NCTM/MENC, etc.—Acronyms of names of professional educators' organizations in various disciplines or interest groups. Most originated in the Progressive Era and remain involved in defining professional practice, promoting educational policy and evaluating educational programs.

Operational definition—Defining something by its actions, rather than by its characteristics or traits. In scientific circles, actions are referred to as "operations."

Potemkin village—A false, but impressive, façade put over or in front of something not so impressive on its own terms. The name's reference is to a supposed incident in Russian history involving a government minister named Potëmkin. The two concepts of reification and Potemkin village reinforce one another in modern educational policy.

Primer—A short introduction to a subject, or a short book designed to teach children to read. Sometimes, analogically speaking, it is a short informational piece.

Progressive—Drawing on the significant political and social initiatives promoted during the Progressive Era of the late 19th an early 20th centuries, a time that transformed the final feudal elements in the world into modern republics. In education, the Progressive Education Association was the main vehicle for promoting democratic and scientific teaching practice. Progressives use scientific research, democratic processes, and innovative technologies to continuously evolve society.

Reify—To reify something means to treat an abstraction as if it were a material or real thing, as in the slogan, "Progress is our most important product." The two concepts of reification and "Potemkin village" reinforce one another in modern educational policy.

Standardized testing—A test designed to compare members of a group consistently and reliably. One of the basic mechanisms of a meritocracy, a system of government where decisions on opportunity and social position are based on demonstrated ability or "merit." In the U.S., standardized testing is best known through the college admissions tests administered by the two large testing companies American College Testing (ACT) and Educational Testing Service (the SAT examination). Both organizations provide standardized testing instruments for everything from elementary school skill testing to medical school admissions testing.

Uncontrolled variable—In scientific experiment, a variable is something that can assume different values. The researcher attempts to control variables so that the only uncontrolled variable is the one he is trying to measure. In educational psychology, the uncontrolled variable is usually the learning task performed by the learner. Unless a teacher is performing a minimal function in the lesson or is completely removed from the scenario, the teacher functions as an additional uncontrolled variable. The teacher variable then skews or distorts the findings of the experiment. This experimental design problem explains why educational psychologists prefer to study individual learners using limited tasks, materials, and experiences.

Worldview—A term that indicates a comprehensive conception of the world, presented as an organic whole, from a particular point of view.

CHAPTER TWO

The Definitions of Pedagogy: The Structures of Teaching

One way to enhance the meaning of a complex topic is to employ metaphorical or analogical thinking to assist us in understanding. Commonly, analogical and metaphorical thinking are reflected in any number of our commonsense elocutions. We learn by heart. We work like a dog. We sing like a bird. We work on the front lines. It's like pulling teeth to get the kids to do anything. We are rigorous in our thinking. We read deeply and broadly. We see the light. We are called to teach. We coach our students. Metaphors are central to human thinking and consciousness (Black, 1962; Lakoff & Johnson, 1980; Ricoeur, 1977; Taylor, 1984).

Our commonsense metaphors and analogies also reveal some of our biases: saying that we work on the front lines sees schools as battlegrounds rather than places of learning. Sometimes we use inconsistent metaphors, and that points to some inconsistency in our thinking: At one of the original Disney-sponsored American Teacher Awards ceremonies, the grand prizewinner, pointing at other teacher award recipients, said, "They're the soldiers, the kids are the troops, and there is a war out there to be won" (Hemion, 1992).

The war metaphor also provides the often heard "in the trenches" image. In this Disney case, though, the teacher did not see the students as enemies, but could not bring himself to see teachers as officers leading their troops. He wanted to be seen as one with the other troops, the students, though the distinction between "soldiers" and "troops" is unclear and, by using different labels, he certainly meant to distinguish between teachers and students. It is interesting that he could accept the war metaphor for education, but not the military leadership connections that follow. One supposes the teacher could have been warring against corporate trends in schooling, or conservative trends, but then he was accepting a trophy from a major corporation that has had some problems with discrimination in the past (they also stopped giving teacher awards in 2006). Maybe he was warring against liberalism. It seems unclear what he meant, though it likely resonated with many who heard him speak.

As with this example, many metaphors and analogies actually trivialize or confuse the topic. In the war metaphor for teaching, no matter who—the student or the administration or the culture—is the logical "enemy," to characterize any of these as an enemy does not lead to better teaching practice. Or, take another example, speaking of teaching as "missionary" work treats students in poor communities (the only population for whom we use this metaphor) as "natives," as the uncivilized "other," and places the teacher in a colonial model of privileged status and benign oppression. In another example, speaking of the brain as a "hard drive" undermines understanding of the complexity of the human brain and the possibilities for teaching (Taylor, 1984).

To employ a somewhat more useful analogy, the field of archaeology can be used suggestively as a means for structuring and understanding ideas regarding pedagogy. The rationale here is both to present some analogical thinking (with clarifying examples) and to provide a heuristic for understanding the complexity of pedagogy. The analogy is not meant to simplify, but merely to illustrate using one of the central features, and central metaphors, of archaeology, namely, the "dig." The dig can be used as a scaffold to discuss pedagogy, though that expression itself looks like a mixed metaphor.

Scaffolding
In psychology, scaffolding is a temporary social or intellectual support provided by a teacher to assist a child in learning.

But the metaphor of **scaffolding**, drawn from Russian psychologist Lev Vygotsky, seems to fit the archaeology analogy: archaeologists use scaffolding just as builders do, and

Metaphor/analogy
Normally a figure of speech where one word or phrase stands in for another to create new images or enrich ideas.

in a way similar to the more common analogical use of scaffolding within cultural psychology as a temporary cognitive structure. Many thinkers have used archaeology as a **metaphor** for complex layering; most famously, Sigmund Freud equated the layers of consciousness to the archaeology of the Roman Forum in *Civilization and Its Discontents* (1930). Actually, many of the archaeologist's digs are "above ground," digging into mounds of earth. These mounds of earth are called "tells," a term of Middle Eastern origin. Aesthetically, James Michener used the tell image to structure *The Source,* his historical novel in which he tells the story of the history of Israel over the millennia (1965).

In smaller Middle East towns, many times one can see a hill just outside the city limits. To the uninitiated, to the nonprofessional, the hill looks natural. For most people, an archaeological *tell* would be perceived as a geological feature, that is, a *hill.* The people in the town next to the hill, those who have some experience of it or have heard stories about it, know that it is a remnant of a previous settlement. However, they do not see into it, they do not learn anything from it that has not been told to them through local lore. They do not know how many layers it has, how old it is, and who lived there before them.

Even those who understand the tell as evidence of an earlier civilization rarely connect the dots to understand that they are also living on a tell in the making, with previous settlements buried beneath them. Maybe they find an artifact that has been exposed or dug out from the surface, but they do not know what the artifact "signifies." Only the professional archaeologists digging into the mound know what lies beneath the layers, and only the professional can sort out the meaning of the artifacts they find through scientific testing and correlation with historical and cultural evidence.

Human history and culture is always built on top of its past: York Minster, the great medieval cathedral in England, is built over the Roman military headquarters; the crypt of its sister cathedral in Ripon is constructed out of Roman tombstones. In our own hemisphere, we also live on the remnants of the past. In downtown Manhattan, workers "discovered" an African American burial ground while digging foundations for a new federal building. In cases where bones are uncovered in New York

City, the first person called is a policeman. Only after various authorities make the determination that no foul play was involved and that the bones come from a past graveyard, are the archaeologists brought into investigate. From the evidence, it appeared that a lost part of New York City's history was coming back into the thoughts of the living. The early history of New York City needed to be rewritten based on the artifacts; all the politics of slavery and history of racism that erased the memory of these founding members of the community were pushed aside and the historical views of pioneer New Yorkers transformed.

In much the same way, pedagogical practice is a tell. Most people appear to think teaching is "natural" when they observe teachers teaching. In fact, the better a teacher is, the more natural teaching seems. Those nonprofessional observers, who normally recognize that they could not teach themselves, might still think that teaching is a special calling and teachers have something "special" about them. Teachers are born, not made, they rhapsodize. The Middle Eastern people who live next to a tell frequently associate it with something spiritual or special or magical as well.

Some teachers themselves, somewhat proudly, may argue that teaching is natural and that they are born teachers. Some assert they have been *called* to teaching by a sense of higher purpose or by a desire to promote social justice. Of course, much as the modern city dwellers living next to the tell are enacting age-old rituals, teachers in schools are doing what was passed on to them from the people who lived in the preceding layers in the pedagogical tell. It is only the teacher who takes on the metaphorical role of the archaeologist who can learn anything new from the mound, and conversely, it is only those who have the ability and knowledge to dig who have the possibility to learn. Those who live only on the surface of the tell of pedagogy are not in control of their own destinies and are less likely to unlock any mysteries for their students about the world at large.

Schema theory/Prior knowledge
The idea that the human brain organizes information by codifying experience. Prior knowledge refers to the current codification of experience in the brain (i.e., its mental schema).

Much of what we observe and perceive is based on what we know and believe—a notion reinforced by **schema theory**, a revolutionary concept derived from cognitive science research. Someone once said that if William Wordsworth, the great poet of 19th-century English Romanticism, had seen the Paleolithic cave paintings at Alta Mira in Spain, he would have interpreted them as the crude expression of the contemporary peasants of the region, rather than as the high art of a prehistoric civilization. It is also worth noting that in 1880 (a year after the cave's discovery) a mainstream scientific meeting ridiculed the **Paleolithic** origin hypothesis; the paintings were not accepted as anything other than modern until after the start of the 20th century and not until evidence from other discoveries and digs were produced. The scientists were no more able to accept the findings than a Romantic poet, but the scientists had a means to correct the perception.

Paleolithic
Old Stone Age, a label coined in 1865, referring to the period in which humans used stone tools.

Importantly, Wordsworth lacked knowledge of prehistory but, more importantly, was committed to the Romantic notion of simplicity allegedly implicit in rural living—a notion we carry in our cultural perceptions to this day. Rural simplicity, for example, is at the heart of the continuing attachment to the myths of the one-room rural schoolhouse, anachronously embodied in many urban small school proposals (Anderson & Summerfield, 2004). Unfortunately, policymakers' envisioning of a past, homogeneous America in the little red schoolhouse blinds us to the new global, multicultural world in which we live.

In any case, today everyone from 8 to 80 knows about dinosaurs and cavemen and even complex geological histories such as those described in tectonic plate theories. The "discovery" of prehistory has affected everything from modern art (Picasso's painting style, e.g.), to cosmology, to the third-grade science curriculum (dinosaurs!), to, as we shall see, the entire approach to studying children and organizing schooling. Archaeologists, by digging up the past, have changed our entire worldview. Teachers are required to not only know where we came from, but also to help students—who have appeared in a world that they did not create but which sports a rich and complex history and structure—understand their past. Pedagogy is a tell that we must continue to dig to understand how what we do evolved, what it meant, and how we are living in our time.

We also need to be archaeologists in our study of pedagogy because so much of what we do seems to be predicated on "beliefs" and "intuition" and even on the elusive notion of "character." All of these abstractions, these products of magical thinking, have an historical and intellectual basis, and even a site of origin. We are thinking and doing like those who have gone before us, but without investigation and reflection we are only miming inherited actions and ideas. The pedagogical tell is as old as human existence. Even if we see the bottom layer as only going back to Socrates (the one we know through Plato's dramatic and philosophical dialogues), that is still almost 2500 years to arrive at current practice. Even a committed professional might hesitate to claim pedagogical expertise in any comprehensive manner under those criteria.

Commonsense Definitions of Pedagogy

Some time must be spent on activating prior knowledge, providing some basic historical and philosophical grounding, regarding expectations for the teacher's role and historical definitions of pedagogy. We need to dig into the tell of pedagogy since a set of assumptions lies beneath the surface that needs to be made transparent. As noted, we live in a time of "contested" spaces and topics. One of the most contested in our time is the role of teachers. For the moment at least we need to quiet some of the current cacophony emanating from the popular media regarding U.S. education and calmly look at the official pronouncements. We need to get past some of the assertions that have arrested continuing dialogue about this central function of any complex society.

In introductory remarks to the United States Department of Education's official release of their compilation, *What Works: Research about Teaching and Learning,* President Ronald Reagan said:

> Good teachers still know what good teachers have always known: we don't need a lot of government interference and fancy gimmicks to produce good schools. What we need is to concentrate hard on basic academic subjects and fundamental moral values. (1986)

While the efforts since 1986 have certainly been to focus on basic academic subjects and fundamental moral values, No Child Left Behind has made government more invasive than ever into teachers' and students' day-to-day lives in school. It seems most school districts are now full of "fancy gimmicks," from scripted lessons to small schools to merit pay to annual testing, none of which were generated from the teaching profession. However, much of the current taken-for-granted discussion of teacher education and teaching in schools assumes the same premise put forward by Ronald Reagan: teachers just need to know their "basic" academic subject and teach the students how to behave properly.

Significantly, however, much of the direction in the current "reform" movement has focused on administrative and managerial efforts rather than on pedagogy. President Reagan's comments above, though they accompanied a substantial summary of research on teaching and learning, appear to suggest that teaching is quite simple. Teaching, says the former President, involves merely knowing your subject and being a moral influence on your students. What could be simpler, or more naïve, or more ideological, than that? President Reagan was not naïve, so there must be a political reason for such a reductive description of teachers' work that simultaneously puts the daunting responsibility for students' *fundamental* moral values onto the shoulders of teachers.

But even if one puts politics aside for a moment, it will not solve the problem. In the end, one can best understand the cultural problem of teachers' uncertain status and confused roles by simply looking at the definition of "pedagogy" in the Merriam-Webster (online) dictionary. How much more complicated, or unclear, can this definition of *pedagogy* be: "The art, science, or profession of teaching." Pedagogy can be an "art" *or* a "science" *or* a "profession." In other words, pedagogy can be any one of three fundamentally different things. To repeat, the dictionary defines *pedagogy* as one, two, or all of three competing worldviews. Considering that the artistic and the scientific views of the world are very different, some say in direct competition with one another, for pedagogy to be one or the other seems impossible, at least on the surface.

Modern dictionaries, of course, are not dictators of meaning, but reporters of meaning. I might note, parenthetically, that this change in purpose from *prescriptive* to *descriptive*, first realized in the publication of the 3rd edition of Webster's International unabridged dictionary in 1961, became a major cultural crisis of the early 1960s (Morton, 1994). Most contemporary dictionaries report *usage*, the way people actually use words in talk and text. Given that assumption, the multiple ways of describing and defining pedagogy must be imbedded in everyday discourse. If pedagogy has multiple meanings within everyday discourse, it follows that participants in pedagogy discussions that are not carefully articulated and premised could end up talking at cross-purposes, talking from different sets of assumptions, or talking past one another.

Merriam-Webster further defines pedagogy as a "professional concern." Professional language tends to be technical and limited to the special meanings that members of that particular profession give it. A professional is someone who comprehends the technical language of the field of knowledge as well as its practice, and a profession is, according to the Merriam-Webster, "a calling requiring specialized knowledge and often long and intensive academic preparation."

Professional discourse in many fields is derisively called "jargon" by the general public, but technical language helps make professional communication more effective or simply more efficient. Professional discourse always needs to be translated for a nonprofessional audience. The combined work of Jean Lave and Etienne Wenger on apprenticeships in various crafts and professions is useful here: part of moving away from the novice's "legitimate peripheral participation" in a profession to "expert" status requires the learning of the language and habits of the profession (1991). Jargon is not meaningless, but a type of professional shorthand. Within any profession, the professional language can be incomprehensible to the average citizen: "hematology" and "habeas corpus" are examples of important concepts in medicine and law respectively generally inexplicable to commonsense.

Finally, the use of the word "calling" in the above definition contains religious or spiritual overtones, as in being "called by God." Professions do not deal exclusively in the realm of science, nor are they seen simply as purveyors of an art (not to demean the value of art, but only to suggest that it is only one element of professional knowledge). I suppose most professionals see some sort of spirituality in their work in any case, or at least feel a sense of being part of something larger than the individual. But it does seem unlikely that the essential premise for a state-supported education system, authorized by modern scientific pedagogy, would predicate its legitimization and authority on spiritual or religious grounds. And yet, quite a few people seem to enter teaching as a "calling."

On the evidence of even this rather terse dictionary definition, *pedagogy* appears a sophisticated concept, requiring some significant study for understanding. Merriam-Webster additionally refers the reader to a secondary meaning of the word *education* for a further definition of pedagogy: "The field of study that deals mainly with methods of teaching and learning in the schools." This definition is the more limited definition of pedagogy, more site-specific and functional. Pedagogy could, one supposes, be limited to teaching in schools, but that definition seems *too* functional. The definition of pedagogy may be in the conflation, or in a reciprocal arrangement, of all three worldviews: the *art* and the *science* and the *profession* of teaching. A look at the history and development of these approaches to the pedagogy question might help us understand better, since it does seems that pedagogy is clearly constructed out of all three of these competing visions.

Some would say that teaching does not vary by discipline except in superficial ways. We as teachers inform students, engage them in learning experiences, and show a passion for our subject field as well as for our students' learning and growth. But those parts of teaching are only the surface of pedagogy, the outward and visible signs, dictated mostly by cultural, social, political, and institutional choices. One must be a skillful practitioner, but that does not define the heart of pedagogy, because pedagogy is always about teaching *something*. And that *something* is not always the same thing—whether it is a discipline, a skill, or a worldview.

Information processing
A metaphor for thinking originating with researchers using computer modeling in cybernetics and cognitive science.

Too much of educational research is clearly aimed at teaching in the abstract, mostly focused on teaching trivial "information" to enhance the statistical reliability of the study. The new paradigm of cognitive science treats thinking as **information processing**, a computing analogy, because much of that research is performed with computer models rather than real people (Rumelhart & McClelland, 1986). The most sophisticated work relevant to pedagogy generally rejects strict behaviorist and information-processing models as inadequate to the task of describing human behavior and cognition. However, the best thinkers about education do not dismiss this research outright but instead keep in mind its limitations and its analogical purpose.

Cultural psychology
Assumption that thinking is affected by cultural as well as biological factors.

Situated cognition
The idea that knowledge is determined by context and the learner's intentions.

The academic field now described as **cultural psychology**, along with the culturally transformed fields of anthropology and sociology, provides many of the new insights for classroom teachers today. However, the paradigm-shifting notion of **situated cognition** comes to us through artificial intelligence research, filtered through cognitive psychology and transformed by social and cultural contextualizing. The idea of "communities of practice,"—one of the more powerful notions about the social nature of knowledge, and its situated-ness—emanated as an analogy with distributed systems of information processing (Wenger, 1999). Psychology, in whatever form, continues to play a central role in pedagogy.

Also worth noting is that the well-worn saw, attributed to Dewey, "learn *by* doing" is better understood, in a reformulation borrowed from Etienne Wenger, to mean "learn *in* doing." The vulgar version of "learn by doing" suggests that learning occurs after you "do," that is, as a result of doing. "Learning in doing," that is, learning as you engage in the task or idea, is more accurate—more dynamic and continuous. The first has become a mechanistic, product-oriented vision; the second maintains its fluidity and progressive elements. One of Dewey's greatest quotations, "Education is not a preparation for life; education is life itself," suggests that he was never confused about the meaning himself. By the bye, this quote, regularly cited, is almost never source referenced by writers; though Dewey says something similar to this quote in *My Pedagogic Creed* (1897) the actual source is unclear. However, this Deweyan formulation of learning is consistent with materialist, evolutionary, or scientific thinking that is now part of modern "commonsense," except, it seems, when applied to schooling.

Child-centered Definitions of Pedagogy

Child-centered
Educational practice focused on a developmental approach.

And, certainly, the great intellectual contribution of psychology was the introduction of **child-centered** or developmentally focused teaching. There were 18th- and 19th-century precursors such as Rousseau, Pestalozzi, and Montessori, all advocating a shift of focus to Nature common in the thinking of the Romantic Movement. But it was psychology in the 20th century that, fully and finally, focused teaching on child-centeredness. In fact, John Dewey's first book was entitled *Psychology* (1887). Dewey's overall influence on schooling can be seen in the placement of psychology at the center of research on learning, and in the argument that democratic societies needed democratic school practices and democratically oriented teachers guided by the wisdom of science.

All of Western society has become scientific in the past several centuries, creating the new physical and social sciences and transforming the way we think about society since the Enlightenment (the years encompassing the end of feudalism and the growth of nationalism). Interestingly, a continuing critique from the intellectual Left accuses Dewey of placing too much faith in science. Dewey belonged to the great American philosophical school of **Pragmatism** ("If a tree falls in the forest and no one is there to hear it, does it make a sound?" No, if you are a Pragmatist.). Dewey was shaped by materialism and pragmatism, both of which preferred an emphasis on science as the source of all answers—an emphasis that continues even today in many areas of U.S. society. The U.S. Department of Education's Institute for Educational Sciences' mission statement, for example, asserts that no knowledge other than "scientific" knowledge will be considered valid for discussions of educational practice.

Pragmatism
Testing hypotheses against real world or practical consequences as a condition of truth and rejecting abstract forms of metaphysics.

Despite recent attempts to make Dewey unique, to either raise him to saintliness or accuse him of inspiring cult-like "liberal" cultural aberrations, there were many more psychologists and sociologists behind the modern child-study and democratic schooling movements encompassed in the Progressive Era. Psychologist G. Stanley Hall essentially "invents" adolescence with his two-volume study, entitled *Adolescence*, published in 1908. Prior to the "invention" of adolescence, one went to elementary school for eight years and then one became an adult and went to work or moved on to high school in preparation for college. "Junior high schools" were developed in response to the "problems" of the undiscovered needs of this "new" population of adolescents. It is noteworthy that some of the current administrative reforms, looking back at the good-old days perhaps, include new K-8 schools. In any case, issues surrounding adolescence have defined elements of Western society in the 20th century, from juvenile delinquency to popular music to sex education.

Adolescence was a new **developmental** stage, "development" being the other great epiphany of psychology in the Progressive Era. Development as a concept arose out of Darwinian thought regarding natural selection and the development of the human species, heretofore allegedly unchanged since the Garden of Eden was created in 4,305 BCE in the most literal religious explanation. (See Stanley Kramer's 1960 film version of Lawrence and

Developmental
A psychological and educational assumption that humans grow and change over time in ways that can be studied and understood.

Lee's play *Inherit the Wind* for the dramatic version of the argument within the context of the Scopes monkey trial). The Darwinian perspective, following a romantic form of naturalism, saw the development of the individual as a recapitulation of the development of the human race. "**Phylogeny recapitulates ontogeny**" was the slogan of the day. Little kids were primitives, just like the "natives" that early anthropologists such as Margaret Mead were studying in the South Seas. "What was 'natural' for primitives?" was the question used to reorganize the elementary school curriculum.

Phylogeny recapitulates ontogeny
The proposition that the embryonal development of an individual organism (its ontogeny) followed the same path as the evolutionary history of its species (phylogeny).

Behavioral scientists of the time took the Darwinian theories to mean that humans, like the rest of the fauna on the planet, were animals. They thought it possible to study animal behavior—a more primitive and, therefore, easier form of behavior to study—and apply it to the understanding of complex human behavior. E. L. Thorndike (1874–1949), the man who popularized educational psychology as a discipline and trained many of the founders of the discipline, studied the behavior of cats before shifting the focus of his study to school children in *Education: A First Book* (1912). Some of the more notorious **sociobiologists** of recent years, such as E. O. Wilson, have spent lifetimes studying creatures such as ants (in Wilson's case) and then making sweeping arguments about human development and behavior (1998). Sometimes this naturalistic approach to human understanding was beneficial, emphasizing the whole child and promoting physical education, for example, and sometimes it could be disastrous, creating enthusiasm for eugenics up until World War II that led to all sorts of human rights abuse, for example.

Sociobiology
A form of Darwinian theory that assumes that human action is the same as other animal actions, and that human characteristics can be explained in terms of evolutionary advantages of certain behaviors.

Child-centeredness in American culture in the 20th century is not just a phenomenon in education, and that is why it is so confusing given the recent neoconservative attacks on child-centered classrooms. The same neoconservatives who appear to denigrate child-centeredness in schooling (decrying social promotion and positive reinforcement, e.g.) push laws that protect children from any number of social shibboleths, from sexual predators to abusive parents, from mass media to drinking and smoking. In a rhetorical parallel, it appears as if neoconservatives, in their complaints about child-centered teaching, are trying to protect children *from* teachers. Not unimportantly, the sexual predator accusation threat implicit in protecting students from teachers may correlate with the significant reduction in the number of men entering elementary school teaching in the past twenty-five years.

It must be the values represented by child-centeredness that conservatives object to, but what values are those, and how do teachers violate children's rights and futures by engaging in child-centeredness? The objection relates to teaching children values rather than subjects, as it is frequently formulated. It is the eternal debate, articulated above by Cavelli-Sforza, between what is learned at home and what is learned at school. The now defunct attempt to teach **values clarification** in the 1970s has the distinction of being the initial target in the current reform movement that seeks to focus schooling on a common core academic curriculum. And, to reference President Reagan's comments above, "fundamental moral values" are not subject to discussion or clarification. And neither is "2 + 2 = 4" in the views of conservative reactionaries.

Values clarification
Educational practice asserting that people make decisions based on their core values which can discovered and refined through discussion.

The opposite of child-centered teaching, or at least the other end of the spectrum, is **subject-centered** teaching (also called "content-based" or "discipline-based" teaching). Proponents of content-based teaching argue that education is the acquisition of information and that the information to be learned is in the traditional disciplines. These policy thinkers tend to object to a variety of things taught outside of "content," including most extracurricular activities.

The sleight of hand here is that the definition of "extracurricular" is problematic. Anything that is considered important can be curricular, rather than outside the legitimated curriculum. The conservative argument demands that anything outside of the traditional disciplines be, by definition, extracurricular and, therefore, outside of the scope of the teacher's responsibilities and the public's interest. This formulation is certainly a logical construct, but an idea that is false at its premise—as many "logical" solutions in education tend to be.

Subject-centered
A curricular focus privileging the subject matter over the child's interests.

Logic rarely has much value in designing human learning experiences. *How We Think* (1910) Dewey's most transformative book, distinguishes between organizing the school curriculum and learning experiences either *logically* and *psychologically*. The child-centered developmental approach, the source of this key organizational distinction, embodied the root of the transformation of

20th century school curriculum and pedagogy. Both the scope and the sequence of the curriculum also change by shifting from the logical to the psychological mindset.

The psychologically organized curriculum planner looks for what is "natural" for a second grader's performance, rather than merely breaking a subject field down logically into its component parts and teaching the "simplest" parts first. Unfortunately, the seemingly simplest part of a subject is one that developed late in the history of the subject. Some examples of seemingly simple ideas that are quite sophisticated are the concepts of "zero" in mathematics, punctuation in grammar, the separation of powers in social studies, and the periodic table in science. All of these can be organized into simple rules and charts, but none of them represents simple concepts. We now call this naturalistic approach "developmentally appropriate."

One of Dewey's greatest critics was Mortimer Adler (1902–2001), who was particularly unhappy with what he perceived as the influence of *How We Think* on school practice. In opposition to the new process models of teaching, Adler formulated the modern concept of *The Great Books* (1990), a compilation of writings that purport to identify and trace the "Great Conversation" of Western culture (Hutchins, 1952). During his long life, he also produced the *Paideia Proposal* during the 1980s flurry of education reports (1982; 1983). Note that he used the ancient Greek term *Paideia* for his curriculum proposal, which referenced an ancient Greek ideal of education. One can see that his proposal contains a humanist manifesto right in the title.

Adler, a lawyer and a philosopher from the traditional humanist school, argued specifically that modern progressives were neglecting "content" for "method." In other words, he believed that John Dewey (and his followers in the Progressive Education Association and their descendants in the Aquarian Revolution of the 1960s) had done great harm to education by shifting curricular emphasis from the content of the curriculum to the developmental needs of the child. Adler argued that the essential ideas necessary to democracy could all be found in his historical selections compiled for the *Great Books* curriculum. Those readings should take precedence over any other curricular matter, especially those of a contemporary nature. Unfortunately, focused as it was on the golden ages of history, Adler's *Great Books* texts excluded all female voices and begrudgingly added a few persons of color to a revised edition in the 1990s.

However, for someone interested only in the content of the curriculum, Adler seemed to want to control the process of education as well. With Charles Van Doren, he wrote *How to Read a Book,* describing the proper way to read and engage in the "great conversation" around *The Great Books.* In this manual for reading, Adler and Van Doren describe what most students since will recognize as study reading, with note-taking, summarizing, and the like, to efficiently get to the "main idea" of the text (1940/1966).

In response to *How to Read a Book,* the literary critic I. A. Richards wrote *How to Read a Page,* a treatise on "close reading" associated with modern literary approaches to reading that have since become normalized critical and analytical reading models (1942). Embodied in the two books is the central debate over the relationship of language and thought in learning. Is language simply a medium, a poor transmitter of thought (ask a mathematics teacher about that idea), or is thought represented in the language itself? The discussion is further clouded today by the recognition of multimodal learning and multimedia representation, and the brouhaha over whole language in opposition to phonics. Still, a position on language and thought needs to be sorted out pedagogically in every classroom.

The Two Cultures of Pedagogy

And, so, even the most content-based educational thinkers always posit an implicit notion of pedagogy, though most of these proposals seemingly take a lecture and discussion pedagogy for granted in articulating arguments for the content of the curriculum. It does not seem unusual then that, for such a seemingly limited view of teaching and culture, the *Paideia Proposal* was the only 1980s education proposal that articulated actual pedagogy. The *Paideia Proposal* required three types of teaching to accompany its *Great Books*:

1. large group lecture (to provide information, i.e., cultural knowledge, to serve as prior knowledge for developing skills and concepts).
2. small group activities to practice intellectual skills and academic habits.

3. small seminars (the pinnacle of the Paideia model) in which the teacher would engage students in a Socratic (ancient Greek, again) discussion of the Big Ideas of Western culture.

This humanist model is still influential, with the *Paideia Proposal* serving as the pedagogical model for Theodore Sizer's Coalition of Essential Schools program. The basic vision of Paideia is also found in the grand humanistic model represented (in much more prosaic fashion) in the "cultural literacy" emphasis in most of the neoconservative curriculum proposals (formerly called "cultural heritage"). Of course, the humanist model has strong proponents within the liberal educational models as well—what differs tends to be the cultural knowledge considered most important, with liberal proposals focusing on contemporary culture and promoting multicultural voices in reaction to neoconservatives' historically remote homogeneous culture focused on mostly European traditions. It is also significant that the content-based curriculum tends to be focused on a more limited knowledge range than the process approaches; Sizer's version of the humanistic model is based on what he calls a "less is more" philosophy, for example, covering less content, but more "deeply" (*Horace's Compromise,* 1985).

But, as noted above, very few educational proposals are overtly anti-humanist. The only thinkers who appear actually anti-humanistic are some of the more radical educational psychologists, purveyors of operant behaviorism or artificial intelligence models, and some of the more radical leftists who consider art to be "bourgeois" and history and culture to be "false consciousness." Many former Marxist thinkers now go by various other politically acceptable labels, some hiding their proposals as feminist pedagogy or critical pedagogy, but remain as deterministic as any other extreme doctrinaire thinking. Authentic feminist pedagogy and functional critical pedagogy are open to possibility and are not generally oppressive or deterministic in their doctrines.

Despite the attraction of humanism, the humanistic approach to education has taken a serious beating in the 20th century, mostly from the new scientific approaches, but also from those who consider humanism to be culturally elitist and exclusionary. The challenge from science as the current dominant worldview accounts for the first. The humanistic tradition's historical roots as "education for the rich" (the education of the elite classes) and continued use as the content for "leadership" education account for the second perception. Strangely enough, the neoliberal position on education also places the arts and humanities strictly in the realm of leadership education, a noblesse oblige consideration for our future leaders. Neoliberalism, though, is also pushing to bring "vocational" education back for the "working classes," a category that was erased in the neoconservative counterrevolution of the past twenty or so years. Neoconservatives think that "vocational" education should exist only as a postsecondary "proprietary school" opportunity.

The humanistic model, heavily focused on rhetoric and philosophy, drove all secular education until the Darwinian revolution of the second half of the 19th century. During this time, the physical sciences took their place as high status knowledge, especially after the tycoons of the Gilded Age started founding "new" universities such as Stanford, MIT, Carnegie Mellon (originally Carnegie Institute of Technology), and the University of Chicago, all with strong science and technology programs. The scientization of culture also invented one of the signature arenas of modern culture— the social sciences. This great educational transformation of schooling came along with the sweeping nationalistic movements of the 19th and early 20th centuries. One could say the social sciences represented a truly scientific, that is, empirical, approach to humanism. As for the change in the politics of the old "let them eat cake" feudal approach, the new nation states needed state-supported school systems to produce a unified citizenry for national pride and mutual defense. Where better to look than the scientific ideas that made these countries great industrial and imperial nations?

In fact, one could argue that the scientific and social revolutions of the 19th century were originally humanistic, but nationalism slipped into colonialism and science was employed to justify all sorts of social wrongs. Much of the impulse for the Romantic revolution of the 19th century, and the aesthetic and humanistic revivals in the 20th, had been a protest against industrialization and technology as spawned by science. And certainly, various scientific-technical trends such as eugenics, artificial intelligence, social efficiency, and utilitarianism seem to degrade the "human" in the term "human being."

This transformation of 20th century culture by science (and its pragmatic form, technology) is also at the root of the distinction between the "art of teaching" and the "science of teaching." The "art of teaching" position is a humanistic argument. The humanistic position is responsible for the development of the first schoolbooks (so-called scholar's editions), the most famous being those of 17th-century Venetian printer Aldus Manutius. The Aldine editions look almost exactly like the books used today, right down to the Garamond fonts and the quarto size (both made possible by the new technology of the printing press). The art of teaching assumes that teaching is based on established historical practices and tied to the transmission of the received culture, the traditional common culture, by skilled artisans. The "art of teaching" side of the debate normally rejects psychology and child study, blaming it for making the curriculum less "rigorous" and for putting the interests of the child ahead of the culture and society.

Science in education, with the introduction of educational psychology at the turn of the 20th century, grows in its influence on school and society with the scientific management studies of the first part of the Progressive Era. Two central studies of the early 20th century still obsess U.S. culture: the time/motion (i.e., social efficiency) studies of Frederick Taylor (1911), and sociologist E. A. Ross's work (1901) on "social control." Taylor was concerned with getting the most out of laborers' time, and Ross's work drew on Americans' fears about the effects of immigrants' "foreign ideologies" on U.S. culture. Social science is also responsible for some of the most liberalizing elements in education thinking. Social science, in the broadest sense, can count any number of school practices in its basket, from testing to counseling, from science laboratories to school nurses, school administration to individualized instruction, ability tracking to school lunch, phonics to sex education.

Science in education is represented by some key trends in social science and by some titanic figures in our intellectual history. Edward L. Thorndike, already discussed, pioneered child study methods and learning theory models and trained most of the first generation of educational psychologists in the United States. Like Noah Webster and other influential school reformers, he left his name on central pieces of the school, including the

Thorndike-Barnhart dictionary, a "school" dictionary built on scientific principles (1997). Others, such as Louis Terman, the developer of the I.Q. test, established psychometrics as the core of the democratic meritocracy. I. A. Richards, the great English literary scholar, even tried to develop a scientific approach to literary reading to account for Cambridge University students' reading deficiencies in *Practical Criticism* (1929). To this day, most of the important decisions about children's success (or failure) are based on or justified by standardized testing that receives its legitimation from behavioral research and psychometric interpretation.

The development of psychometrics from the early I.Q. testing experiments is also one of the defining elements of school practice in the U.S., virtually defining the democratic concept of "meritocracy." Intelligence tests, and later, achievement tests represented by the SAT, ACT, and recent **NCLB** efforts, were used to sort the students into academic tracks based on predicted academic potential. In other words, students were tracked into more efficiently organized classes along with their intellectual peers, with the assumption that they would also be better prepared for their eventual place within the culture. The workers, the technicians, the managers, and the leaders would all receive appropriate educations, each necessarily different form one another. As suggested above, one of the great triumphs of the neoconservative revolution has been the elimination of formal tracking, the assertion of a single curriculum, and the movement of vocational and technical education to the postsecondary, proprietary schools, arguably a much more "democratic" curriculum.

ESEA/NCLB
The Elementary and Secondary Education Act (1965) was the first major funding of public education by the federal government. The 2001 reauthorization of ESEA, No Child Left Behind, made state funding contingent upon agreeing to federal accountability standards.

Another important figure in psychology that also deeply affected school policy was B. F. Skinner (1904–1990), the behavioral scientist. Skinner described his Utopia in his book *Walden Two*, in which he imagined the salutary result of implementing his behavioral psychology (1948). In recent years, the cybernetic movement and artificial intelligence have dominated the philosophical discussion, most of which is simply an extension of Skinner's key insights regarding the human animal and his deep conviction that all meaningful human learning was strictly a matter of stimulus and response within the organism. Skinner's work shaped much of the "individualized" learning curriculum instituted in schools after WWII (SRA Reading kits, e.g.) and still provides the intellectual basis for most of the individualized learning currently in schools. The most important critique of Skinner and the scientific model of human research, especially the dangers of the machine metaphor, was by the humanist psychologist Carl Rogers (1902–1987). In an essential essay in *On Becoming a Person,* Rogers unmasks the basic mechanical (i.e., cybernetic) nature of the behaviorist paradigm (1961).

All of these cognitive science models use machine metaphors for evoking human thinking and normally tend to try to "teacher proof" the curriculum ("teacher proof" is a linguistic parallel with "idiot proof"). The individualized learning ideal replaces the teacher with a tightly controlled, self-regulating system. Behavioral sciences, especially educational psychology, have always argued that teaching should be driven by the ways in which children learn, and that teachers are always interfering with that process. Much of behavioral research struggles to reduce the "teacher variable" in learning studies, as if the teacher confounds the problem of student learning rather than assisting in the processes. The current infatuation with script-based teaching represents another attempt to teacher proof the lesson.

Science has continued to dominate the basic discussions of teaching and learning, though teacher lore dominates teacher lounges and the social and cultural functions of schooling remain at the center of the political debate across the entire spectrum of political beliefs. The direction of some of this behavioral research appears sensible, if you believe that learning is about efficiency, that is, about learning *more, faster*. It also appears sensible if you believe that learning is just what happens in the biological organism. As teachers, we already know that the teaching experience in the classroom involves more than modifying the stimuli to positively (or negatively) reinforce the learned response. What we do is pretend that the researchers do not know what they are talking about and go back to the tried-and-true ways of running our classrooms. We also know that the political pressures of teaching, reinforced by administrators and parents, are much more pressing that the intellectual contempt we risk from researchers far away in the universities. None of this is too good for the research and practice relationship.

Much of "scientific" research is not very sophisticated. Merely performing a statistical analysis does not make something "scientific." Also, the original numbers in many psychometric studies, mostly rating scales, have nonnumeric characteristics or criteria. What does it mean to say that John or Maria scored a 5 on a test of standard written English? What were the criteria on which they were judged to add up to a 5, or be rated a 5? Statistics has also produced the assumption that the whole world is represented by a "bell curve" where most people are, by definition, counted average or normal, and we spend most of our time measuring ourselves and our students against a mean distribution (Herrnstein & Murray, 1994; Kincheloe, Steinberg & Gresson, 1997).

More importantly, teachers frequently find themselves on the short end of a meaningless statistic that is used to indict their performance. Policymakers are not above using statistics to skew data. The Texas "school miracle" of the 1990s was later found to be based on falsified and incomplete data (Helfand, 2000). Nineteenth-century British prime minister Benjamin Disraeli (one of many believed to be the author of the phrase) said there were three types of lies, "lies, damn lies, and statistics." Famed British IQ researcher Cyril Burt was found to have falsified much of the data on his twin studies that purported to demonstrate the superiority of nature in the nature versus nurture argument, using both statistics and deception.

However, regardless of these circumstances, we *do* care about the research findings of behavioral science. Behavioral science, in particular educational psychology, has taught us how positive reinforcement is superior to punishment, something seemingly central to the older teaching traditions. Behavioral science, even when driven by the social efficiency movement, has taught us better ways to engage in various learning activities, such as silent reading and written composition (replacing the grand tradition of oral recitation). Much of what we modern (and postmodern) teachers take for granted about teaching comes from behavioral research. Motivation, assessment, lesson planning, objectives and aims, positive reinforcement, activity-based learning, collaborative learning, and experiential learning are all a result of scientific study in the 20th century. Without scientific research and the technological revolution, we would still be doing recitation in classrooms and reading the New England Primer (1688).

Fortunately, much of the scientific study of education has shifted dramatically in the past generation or so, away from

Cognitivism
The application of quantitative and behavioral science methods to the study of human thinking.

behaviorism and toward **cognitivism**. The concepts of "cognitive schema" and "instructional scaffolding" now central to educational discussions were not part of the behavioral approach at all. As a result, the old debate between humanistic psychology and behaviorism has disappeared from current discussion. Given that the structure of the ideological debate still remains, cultural psychology is presented in opposition to cognitive science. The same argument applies, the cultural psychologists accuse the cognitivists of dehumanizing and de-contextualizing student learning; the cognitivists accuse the cultural psychologists of romanticism and political meddling. And, all of this coincides with the recent emphasis on academic learning to the exclusion of all else in the comprehensive vision of educating children. Cultural psychologists tend to be in the forefront of the criticism of privileging formal academic education for children.

It is easy to forget how abstractly formalized schooling was before modern science. And "scientific" studies continue to shape new practices and reinforce or deny new theories. The problem in scientific study comes when it claims to be about the one and only truth, and that is called "scientism." The local problem is when scientists of all stripes try to reduce teaching to deterministic learning models developed in laboratory settings. I remember one particular draconian reading system from my early years of teaching in which I was supposed to spend a significant amount of time practicing the pronunciation of the *schwa* sound (a phoneme) with my limited proficiency 8th graders. It turned out that the exercises were taking up a lot of class time that could be used for actual reading, something these kids had been deprived of since elementary school in favor of sound-letter correspondence lessons. I shifted to a language experience approach in which students engaged in more self-selected reading aimed at fluency enhancement. The reading scores improved, because the "problem" was a lack of language experience rather than inability to match letter with sound. In this case, at least it seemed to me, the "scientific" approach was reducing these students' chances to become readers, not because it was "wrong" but because it was too narrow and restricting regarding the teacher's and students' actions.

Unfortunately, discussion of the teacher knowledge base usually ends in a debate over scientific-based learning theory, especially in political and social policy statements. If one looks at the formal definition of scientific research in the federal "what works" policy algorithm, one will see that control and evaluation is what the federal bureaucrats really want. They admit that much themselves and say that the term "scientific" many times means "evaluation" studies (i.e., what works). What they really mean is not scientific, but functionalist, pragmatic studies of teaching and learning centered on the assumptions embedded in standardized testing.

In other words, instead of truly scientific, empirical study, the U.S. Department of Education means limited, controlled studies of learning based on assumptions of learning they already hold. What are those assumptions? Learning is acquiring information. Knowledge, by which they mean information, can be broken down into manageable parts, but in a hierarchical structure, and taught, invariably, in a particular order and at a particular time in the child's personal development. The students who do not learn in "proper" fashion, and in a specific, limited timeframe, must be punished for their own good until they demonstrate they have learned the information.

That's the description of the new third-grade tests and the rationale for ending "social promotion" in New York City. Given the complexity of the school population in New York City, one would think that the officials would see the limitations in this approach. On the other hand, one can see where reducing all complexity to a simple sequence and then blaming the kids for their "failure" would be a wonderful political solution. It is also a wonderful accountability model, as long as you do not feel accountable to the kids. These are the same neoconservative policymakers who criticize "liberal" teaching methods because they are allegedly too formulaic.

The federal government uses the criteria of the "scientific" model to deny grants to educational researchers who want to pursue other methods and worldviews. Classroom teachers' anger about educational research, usually directed indiscriminately against university education faculty, is likely produced by researchers who claim that it is not their responsibility to translate the work into classroom practice. The contempt that some of this research appears to have for teachers and teachers' abilities is visited upon the teacher education faculty at the universities as much as upon the teachers in the field.

One can see the conflicted worldview played out in the structure of teacher certification. Not much has changed since I graduated from college. I received a Bachelor of Science degree, rather than a Bachelor of Arts, because I was in the teacher education group. I studied the same English courses as those receiving the B.A., in fact I had to complete more English requirements, but I was also studying scientific approaches (i.e., educational psychology) to education. One presumes that the initial distinction of the B.S. from the B.A. for teachers was to place the teachers in the new science knowledge paradigm. The B.S. would be seen as new knowledge, superior to the old. Having studied the same American and English literature as my B.A.-seeking peers (and a few courses in language and composition not required of them), my education would be modified, even transformed, by my additional study of the science of learning. I was a man of science, not a medieval humanist, said the state authorities and the professional organizations.

One can see where those of us in English, the grand dame of all humanistic study, might have some conflicting intellectual paradigms to manage that the science teachers need not spend much time on. The history majors were like the English majors, but many of their peers were majoring in the social *sciences*. C. P. Snow, the British scientist and philosopher, best articulates the conflict between the scientific and the humanistic when he argues that the worldviews of the two positions remain in eternal conflict (*The Two Cultures*, 1959). It was certainly a sizable problem, to say the least, for undergraduates to sort out individually. My peers who stayed the course with the B.A. and did not study educational psychology needed to deal with only one worldview. One can see where the current split between the alternate route and state-certified teachers' skills and attitudes emanates from. One is based on scientific learning; the other is a craft-based humanist model of teaching.

The twist here is that even the most conservative of teachers employ liberal-progressive, scientifically researched learning models in their day-to-day teaching. It is really more a question of whether these approaches are conscious or unconscious. It is interesting to see that most of the neoconservative voices of the 1980s' counterrevolution took for granted many elements of the very doctrine they were attacking. E. D. Hirsch, Jr., spent much of

Cultural Literacy attacking Dewey and the Progressives to argue for a pragmatic approach to classroom learning based on cognitive science. How could the progressives have ever been against that? Hirsch was co-opting an educational psychology model built around schema theory, arguing for scientifically based learning theory and presenting a pragmatic and functionalist philosophy of education. The fact that he was using this approach to argue for a medieval-sounding mentalist curriculum that even Galileo would have found suspect shows how conflicted these issues are at the moment.

In many universities, the conflict of the traditional liberal arts with the new sciences is still reflected in departmental structures: there are different departments for mathematics and applied mathematics in many universities. Educational psychology is rarely found outside schools of education in universities even though the name should clearly tie it with the other psychologies (which themselves are split between experimental and clinical). These are competing paradigms where one has not replaced the other but has been added without reconciliation. On the other side, philosophy has been reduced to analytic philosophy in new departments of cognitive science, and linguistics has been reduced to computational linguists in those same departments. There are very few linguistics and philosophy departments left in colleges outside the traditionally elite ones.

This traditional dualism between scientism and humanism is not helpful to discussions of pedagogy. First, we need to put scientific studies of learning back into their proper perspective. Scientific study of learning and teaching, as represented by educational psychology, is a central a part of pedagogical schema. However, much of the research in our time about *schools* is anthropological and social. One of the reasons for the change has been the clear realization that the very nature of scientific study is limiting in providing "answers" for teachers in classrooms (Jackson, 1968). What teachers are talking about when they talk about "exposing" kids to something is a cross between formalism and behaviorism. In most cases it means experiential learning, as in music appreciation or writing a paragraph. In other cases, it means something more formalistic, such as doing division and multiplication of fractions. In neither case does the notion of "exposure" serve an educative purpose.

The other effect of the hegemony of behavioral research is that so many questions of teaching remain trapped by the tyranny of these learning models. For example, one's identity as a teacher and one's personal perceptions of self are caught up in our "teaching style." There is teacher style as in *Simpsons* creator Matt Groenig's book, *School Is Hell*, which lays out some of the teacher stereotypes we have come to accept and even project onto individual teachers. Archie Comics' Miss Grundy and Dickens' Mr. Gradgrind (*Hard Times*) are traditional stereotypes of teachers more interested in the "facts" than the kids and are potent examples of teachers who destroy the joy of learning for kids. There are examples of "good teachers" as well as "bad teachers," but most of the familiar portraits are hardly flattering to professionals.

The researcher Bruce Joyce and his associates worked hard to make teaching style a central category in the discussion around professional development (Joyce, Weil & Calhoun, 2003). The basic notion is that models of teaching (what he called teaching style) are developed around learning models that either depend on the teacher's notions about kids and learning or fit a particular set of goals or particular material (Huitt, 2003). The first of these learning models is the behavioral systems approach that includes direct instruction and mastery learning (Skinner, Bloom, e.g.). The second is the information-processing approach that has a developmental focus and includes inquiry-based or inductive thinking, concept development, and intellectual development in general (Vygotsky, e.g.). The third approach is the personal development focus that includes student-centered humanistic teaching (Rogers, e.g.), personal awareness and development, and focus on creativity. The fourth model is the social interaction one, including cooperative learning (Slavin, 1989; Johnson & Johnson, 1986) and roleplaying. The scientific perspective, in this case, posits teaching style as simply adopting a set of assumptions about learning styles.

In other words, the teacher becomes merely an application of a particular concept or system from educational psychology. But, even within the teaching styles categories there are many different styles. However, one needs to recognize that the educational psychology model of teaching style does provide us with some important insights. Teachers do require an explicit, articulated model of student learning for their planning and action in the classroom.

The best teachers recognize a full range of learning styles and their attendant teaching styles. Though teachers are not subservient to learning models, we need to be knowledgeable about the findings on student learning, especially in a developmental context.

Professional thinking for classroom teachers needs to reconcile these competing ideas, these inherently contradictory practices, these different ways of living in the world. So, pedagogy begins to shape itself in our thinking: pedagogy is the professional mind-set, the habits of mind, of a teacher arrayed within multiple and diverse forms of reference. A psychological stance, a cognitive schema, and habits of mind influence our actions in classrooms and shape our thinking about the behavior of children. Teachers are able to balance those complexities and teach in a meaningful manner. Or not.

Glossary

Child-centered—A distinction growing out of child study in psychology, in which educational practice is focused on teaching the child, a developmental approach, as opposed to teaching the subject, a logical approach to transmitting specific information. Used in any number of situations, the child-centered approach is always seen as positive in liberal-progressive educational circles.

Cognitivism—Cognitivism is the application of behaviorist methods—that is, quantification, positivism, and scientific method—to the study of human thinking. Both behaviorism and cognitivism are reductionist theories in their assumptions about humans, seeing human thought and behavior as reducible to discrete and identifiable components governed by discoverable rules.

Cultural psychology—A field of psychology that does not believe humans are subject to universal rules and asserts that mind and culture are intertwined. Assumes that thinking is affected by cultural as well as biological factors.

Developmental—A psychological and educational assumption that humans grow and change over time in ways that can be studied and understood. Psychological study of children's developmental has now expanded to adolescent and adult populations.

ESEA/NCLB—The Elementary and Secondary Education Act, established in 1965, was the first major funding of public education by the federal government, created as part of the Great Society and War on Poverty initiatives under President Lyndon Johnson. The National Assessment of Education Progress was added during ESEA's reauthorization in 1969 under President Richard Nixon. The 2001 reauthorization of ESEA, consumer-branded as No Child Left Behind, made state funding contingent upon agreeing to federal accountability standards and employing only "scientific" research for educational study and policy.

Information processing—A computer-based metaphor for thinking originating with researchers using computer modeling in cybernetics and cognitive science. Artificial intelligence and cybernetic research focus on machine intelligence, assuming that humans are machines, and also generalize about human cognition.

Metaphor/analogy—Normally a figure of speech where one word or phrase stands in for another to create new images or enrich ideas: "It's raining cats and dogs" or "The mind is a computer" or "Children are savages." Not all metaphors are helpful to careful thinking, as in all three of the examples here. In rhetoric, an analogy is simply a metaphor that uses "like" or "as." In philosophy, metaphor and analogy can be distinguished as the difference between the "as if" of analogy (useful in social science) and the "as being" of metaphor (poetic or spiritual). There is a world of difference between "A child is like an animal" and "A child is an animal." Sociobiologists might argue that "a child is an animal" is neither metaphorical nor analogical, but "true."

Paleolithic—Old Stone Age, a label coined in 1865, referring to the period in which humans used stone tools. 99 percent of human history occurred in the Paleolithic period, extending from 2.5 million years ago until 10,000 BC.

Phylogeny recapitulates ontogeny—The proposition that the embryonal development of an individual organism (its ontogeny) followed the same path as the evolutionary history of its species (phylogeny). Served as a rationalization, for example, for G. Stanley Hall's maturation theories that promoted the recognition of adolescence as an important stage of human development.

Pragmatism—An American philosophical school whose most famous purveyors include Charles Sanders Pierce, William James, and John Dewey. Pragmatists test hypotheses against real world or practical consequences as a condition of truth, rejecting abstract forms of metaphysics. Pragmatists also assume that thought guides action, the basis for critical thinking, problem solving, and reflective teaching. Frequently confused with the traditional meaning of "pragmatic," which means rejecting intellectual and artistic matters for facts and practical matters.

Scaffolding—In psychology, scaffolding is a temporary social or intellectual support provided by a teacher to assist a child in learning. It is analogous to the function of a construction scaffold, meant to be moved, readjusted, reconstituted, or removed as the situation changes and the building grows.

Schema theory/Prior knowledge—The idea that the human brain organizes information by codifying experience. Prior knowledge refers to the current codification of experience in the brain (its mental schema) and relates to the effect of the current organization on assimilating or rejecting new experience and modifying the mental schema.

Situated cognition—The idea that thinking is always "in the moment" and that knowledge is determined by context and the learner's intentions.

Sociobiology—A form of Darwinian theory that assumes that human action is the same as other animal actions, and that human characteristics can be explained in terms of the evolutionary advantages of certain behaviors. Tends to draw analogies from animal study and focus on discussions of such categories as mating behaviors, pack hunting, and hive activity.

Subject-centered—A curricular focus privileging the subject matter over the child's interests. Frequently, and erroneously, referred to as "teacher-centered."

Values clarification—A theory asserting that people make decisions based on their core values. As an educational method, values clarification assists individuals in articulating and organizing their value systems. Values clarification is subject to criticism for its relativistic approach to values and/or for its liberal bias. Some parents also object to its therapeutic intent in some instances, raising questions of privacy.

CHAPTER THREE

Pedagogical Content Knowledge: Professionalism and Teacher Thinking

Lots of people get paid to teach children in our schools; not every one of them is a pedagogical specialist in a field of study. Some possess degrees in their subject fields, but some do not. Further, what defines a college degree in a major varies by institution. This is true even in elite institutions; some Ivy League institutions require very little in the manner of required courses, while others specify much of the curriculum. Public universities tend toward "requirements" based on menu-style selections that make the actual course content of identical degrees vary from one student to another.

Given this diversity of requirements, and the lack of interest in interfering with college curriculum requirements, the state departments of education normally set minimum academic standards defining teacher certification. Those regulations for certification do not properly address the "problem" of subject matter qualifications of the "well-qualified" teacher required by NCLB or sought by the profession because they do not provide any truly common standards (Darling-Hammond & Bransford, 2005). And, of course, state education authorities and college faculty do not control the professional requirements alone. In addition to the state authorities, professional organizations of teachers were involved in establishing the state curriculum frameworks and are involved in the evaluation of teacher education program approved by various accrediting agencies such as **NCATE**.

NCATE
National Council for the Accreditation of Teacher Education, an accrediting agency for schools, colleges, and departments of education (SCDE).

Recent attempts to broaden the teaching pool in many states have moved more toward the **ways of knowing** perspective, with state certification authorities allowing degreed engineers and business majors to teach mathematics, for example (see Bruner, 1985, for rationale). This adjustment is in response to school districts assigning certified teachers in social studies and home economics to teach mathematics, given the shortage of mathematics graduates who pursue secondary school teaching. Even if there were enough mathematics majors to go around, just possessing a degree in a particular academic discipline does not make one a teaching professional in any case. The state, for one, also requires some pedagogical (or at least teacher training) certification beyond majoring in the subject.

Ways of knowing
An approach to knowledge that emphasizes forms of representation and cognitive processes over knowledge acquisition and recall.

There have been many "reforms" put in place in response to the *A Nation at Risk* report since 1983. The largest were federally funded projects to produce "model" state frameworks for all school subjects and grade levels. The intention was that state departments of education would develop state curriculum guidelines that would, in turn, facilitate standardized testing for the now ubiquitous high-stakes promotion and graduation requirements. The federal government decided against a national testing system as part of a political commitment to federalism and states' rights; the state governors (lead by Roy Romer, Colorado governor and later Los Angeles school superintendent,) generally agreed with the states' rights model of governance and evaluation (Romer & Fitzgerald, 1996).

The second big federal project was to study the status of teacher quality and provide recommendations based on the "best practices" of "expert" practitioners in classrooms across the nation. The biggest project researched what separated the "experts" from "novices" in teaching and was awarded to the well-known researcher Lee Shulman, known for some of the most sophisticated educational research done in the previous generation. The purpose of the study would be to identify *good* teaching (now labeled the **well-qualified teacher**), delineate some of the "best practices," and to see "what works" and what doesn't. The hope

Well-qualified teacher
A set of standards for teacher preparation set by the federal government under NCLB.

was for creating exemplary models of new teacher preparation, and many states used guidelines based on this research to recertify their teacher education programs in the 1990s.

Shulman, named president of the Carnegie Foundation for the Advancement of Teaching in 1998, was a well-known professor of psychology who had contributed to educational thinking for many years through his research on learning. Shulman's research into what makes an effective teacher (what distinguished an **expert** from a **novice**) produced some interesting findings. First, teaching knowledge is domain specific; that is, what an earth science teacher needs to know is different from what a math teacher needs to know. Interestingly enough, the cognitive science research produced during roughly the same period argues that learning a subject is a matter of learning to operate within the conventions of the body of thought (Bruer, 1993).

Novice/expert Distinction in professional study between inexperienced and experienced practitioners.

Shulman also helped transform the research paradigm, recognizing the newer studies and research methods needed to address the real-life elements of teaching necessary to defining good practice:

> Another reason ... is the shift of research paradigms currently underway in our field. We are developing well-reasoned, methodologically sophisticated, and logically argued approaches to the use of qualitative methods and case studies to parallel our already developed approaches of correlational and experimental inquiry. These newer approaches introduce both a new kind of data about which to reason and new modes of reasoning themselves. (1986, p. 12)

The last statement is particularly important, since it suggests that teacher "quality" cannot be accounted for by simple measures of student achievement or "value-added" criteria. Teacher quality is a qualitative measure, and teaching remains a humanistic endeavor regardless of the scientific studies of learning.

There are two really important ideas that come from Shulman's research. The first is that not all of the required knowledge for teaching, or studying teachers, is "scientific" in nature. The second is that cultural expectations exert enormous influence on teachers, regardless of scientific generalizations about learning and development. In one sense, Shulman reopened the question of whether teaching is an art or a science. In the earlier "art versus science" dialogue, most of the "teaching is an art" people were anti–scientific pedagogy and pro–subject matter. What Shulman illustrated was that teaching was indeed an art, but an art that relied on scientific knowledge as well as cultural demands. Teachers chose their curriculum based not on some determining model of individualized learning, but a range of factors weighing the interests of the children and community. Shulman's research also supported both a reflective theory of teaching and an experience-based model of teacher development. Teaching ability is tied to the power of reflection and the achievement of understanding.

When we look at the other important research on teacher experts ("expert pedagogues") completed during that time by David Berliner, another educational psychologist, we see some clear distinctions between the novices and experts:

> It is said that novices in many fields hold literal views of objects and events whereas experts make inferences about those objects and events. It is also said that experts show self-regulatory or metacognitive capabilities that are not present in less mature or experienced learners. (Berliner, 1986, pp. 10–11)

In an interview with Ronald Brandt of ASCD, Berliner elaborates further:

> A characteristic of experts [is that] they have organized knowledge. Experts no longer merely see, they organize what they see into something more meaningful to them. [We tested to see if]...expert teachers can process several sources of specialized information simultaneously. The literature on experts says they should be able to.... The novices...didn't have anywhere near the ability. (Brandt, 1986, p. 7)

Novice teachers, defined by Berliner as teachers who have completed student teaching or one year of teaching, have not learned to be teachers yet. Berliner explains: "novices are concerned with where the holes are, while the experts take off from what kids know. One is a deficit model and the other is a strength model" (Brandt, 1986, p. 7). In other words, all novices exhibited a range of limitations in their teaching, limitations that could be overcome only by developing "self-regulatory and metacognitive capabilities." The question remained: what is the nature, or at least the definition, of these capabilities?

One of the groundbreaking paradigms of Shulman's extensive research findings was what he and his researchers named "pedagogical content knowledge," an amalgam of disciplinary knowledge, knowledge of human development, and craft knowledge that was synthesized by teachers who exhibited "best practices." Dewey's psychological organization of the curriculum, transformed by current disciplinary demands, was reinvented as pedagogical content knowledge and was defined by Lee Shulman as that

> which goes beyond knowledge of the subject matter per se to the dimension of subject matter knowledge for teaching.... Within the category of pedagogical content knowledge I include, for the most regularly taught topics in one's subject area, the most useful forms of representations of those ideas, the most powerful analogies, illustrations, examples, explanations, and demonstrations—in a word, ways of representing and formulating the subject that make it comprehensible to others. Pedagogical content knowledge also includes an understanding of what makes the learning of specific topics easy or difficult; the conceptions and preconceptions that students of different ages and backgrounds bring with them to the learning of those most frequently taught topics and lessons. (quoted in Grossman, 1990, p. 7)

It is certainly possible to read art, science, and craft into the statement regarding teaching knowledge. Some would argue that the above statement is a little too strong on craft knowledge, unless one sees the question of "analogies, etc." as more than examples passed from generation to generation of teachers. One would also assume that the simple use of activities in which one had engaged as a student would not fit the category. Implicit in the above definition, especially the epistemological question of what makes learning something easy or difficult, is knowledge of human development. Shulman is a psychologist, after all.

One of Shulman's associates, Pamela Grossman pursued the question quite thoroughly in one of the better books ever written on teacher development, *The Making of a Teacher: Teacher Knowledge and Teacher Education* (1990). That study's report, which contains the Shulman quote above, investigated the success of six first-year English teachers: three had been taught the structure and beginnings of pedagogical content knowledge within a teacher preparation program, and three began teaching with no teacher preparation. She found that the ability to employ pedagogical content knowledge was an important factor in the success or failure of these beginning teachers. Her definition of pedagogical content knowledge is composed of four "central elements":

> 1. Knowledge and beliefs about the purposes for teaching a subject at different grade levels.
> 2. Knowledge of students' understanding, conceptions, and misconceptions of particular topics in a subject matter.
> 3. Knowledge of curriculum materials available for teaching particular subject matter, i.e., "curricular knowledge."
> 4. Knowledge of instructional strategies and representations for teaching particular topics. (Grossman, 1990, pp. 8–9)

Grossman's definition of curricular knowledge is a content-based one; but implicit in it is the psychologically organized curriculum. Grossman also discourses at some length on the limitations of learning to teach from experience (1990, p. 38). Again, although experience is essential, it is not enough. She concluded that success of these first-year teachers in her study was due to their curriculum design abilities that they developed based on the nascent pedagogical content knowledge they acquired and developed before beginning to teach. Their ability to learn to teach in each classroom setting could be understood within the context of their curricular understanding. Their cognitive scaffolding for learning to teach was essential to their overall learning and development once they entered the classroom.

The operational nature of pedagogical content knowledge is implicit in Grossman's study. The new teachers who were professionally prepared were not just taught to be "more open" but were taught a specific "psychologized" view of the English curriculum. The pedagogical content knowledge for teaching in a "process" manner is a function of these theories. One does not experience the "psychologized" curriculum in the college classroom that supplies the content knowledge—the college knowledge, adult knowledge, is organized "logically." But, pedagogical content knowledge is interconnected with the content of the disciplines, because pedagogical content knowledge functions within a cultural perspective.

What Grossman's work suggests is that the task of learning to teach is even more difficult for those who have no pedagogical content knowledge base. But there is an alternative hypothesis: one cannot learn to teach in a way consistent with progressive, scientific approaches to teaching without pedagogical content knowledge. One can still be a successful teacher using the liberal arts paradigm, but the habits and tacit knowledge will eventually reflect some of the pedagogical content knowledge, especially the craft knowledge elements, simply because of the dictates of classroom teaching. According to Grossman's research, the non-prepared teachers (the alternate route teachers) continue to exhibit "novice" behaviors, like approaching the kids on a deficit basis.

The pedagogical content knowledge model has been criticized as being too "teacher-centered." Advocates of what has been termed "informal education," for example, propose a vision of teaching that is less structured and appear to be focusing on the importance of incidental learning, which cannot be as easily shaped by a teacher's expectation. Informal educators favor more "naturalistic" settings in school learning, normally promoted as "indirect instruction." Some thinkers regard informal education as an extension of the Progressive Era "open education" movement that was reawakened in the 1960s, a movement that promoted student experiences and "self-actualizing" learning. But, even informal education requires a teacher who is self-aware that she is being informal.

To these critics, effective instruction methods based on pedagogical content knowledge is "direct instruction," and not the proper way to address the education of children. But the pedagogical content knowledge approach serves the "visible knowledge" approach to pedagogy, not the direct instruction version. It undermines the secret knowledge view of teaching, though it does put it in the hands of the experts. We currently live in an age where "passion" is accorded more value than expertise. In fact, expertise is often seen as a disqualification for pursuing a reform agenda. Arguing that the less teachers know, and the less they do, makes student learning better simply makes little sense, unless one is ideologically committed to delegitimizing teachers' roles in learning.

Schulman demonstrated that effective teachers, "effective" by more than one measure of success, possess a special knowledge, a knowledge-in-action. It was not enough to have knowledge of the "subject" to teach; one needed to understand the subject in ways that would make it accessible and understandable to learners. Treating kids as remedial adults was not sensible, teaching math in history class was not efficacious, and lack of awareness of "meaning making" in your discipline made teaching concepts particularly difficult. Teachers need to know what they are doing, that is, possess a conscious awareness of their skills and practices in the complex realm of today's classroom.

As criteria, Shulman first asked teachers which colleagues they thought were good teachers for his research team to observe. He studied teachers in every field, at all grade levels, in differing settings, and across the spectrum of preparation and experience. Shulman began with the assumption that there was a professional culture of teaching. In his forthcoming decade-long study of the professions, not troubled by the assertion that teaching is merely a craft rather than a profession, he included teaching as an equal member of the professions. And, he assumed that the history and practices of the profession were worth investigating, rather than rejecting current teaching practice as either outmoded or ideological.

The only serious remaining issue is the question of whether the *expert* teachers were simply replicating their teaching practices year after year or whether the true "expert" was continually evolving and changing. There clearly are teachers who, having gotten 180 perfect lessons together, would probably be judged expert pedagogues. However, it simply defies commonsense that such an approach to expertise could really be possible without some "natural" change overtime. The true expert pedagogue would most likely be in search of novelty and transformation over time, and her own growth as a person and scholar would also be reflected in transformation and change within her classroom.

Teacher Preparation and the Knowledge Base of Teaching

Given the assumption that professional knowledge is implicit in the pedagogical content knowledge formulation, it is necessary to analyze the intellectual structure of teacher preparation and professional development as a means to lay a foundation for the full discussion of pedagogical content knowledge. Many teachers, having completed teacher preparation at a university, have no idea how teacher preparation in a university is intellectually organized. One reason for that predicament is that teacher education is not a unified system of knowledge as it currently stands and, like most other programs (and even majors) in universities, is treated more as a series of courses rather than as a coherent program.

The teacher education system is not "mindless"—to cite a particularly unhelpful formulation from reporter Charles Silberman's 1970 classic *Crisis in the Classroom.* Simply put, the political forces in the state and the intellectual schisms within the university have compromised on a mix of contradictory components to soothe proponents of competing ideologies and to codify legal and professional certification. And, these certification laws have reified the current contradictory conglomeration of courses that we call teacher preparation as if it were the best possible arrangement.

What every teacher preparation "program completer" does know is that the program has three distinct academic parts: educational foundations, educational psychology, and teaching the subject, the latter historically and reductively referred to as "methods." This constitutes the formal professional education component of teacher certification. Teachers are also required to complete courses that meet general and teacher-specific liberal arts requirements and to major in a subject matter discipline.

Elementary education and secondary education teacher preparation are quite different in that elementary teachers require teacher education in all knowledge fields (appropriate to the developmental age of children) because they teach all subjects in self-contained classrooms. Recently, some elementary schools reorganized to include subject teachers who teach only mathematics, for example, to all students of the same grade. Whether all elementary school teaching will mimic secondary and higher education remains to be seen, though it does seem a logical step in dealing with the problem of science and mathematics instruction being undervalued in elementary classrooms. In any case, as a result of the neoconservative arguments against teachers "majoring in education," many states now require a prospective elementary school teacher to major in another academic field as well as complete the major in elementary education. Despite the rhetoric, secondary school teachers have never "majored" in education but pursue academic study consisting of the same major (usually with additional, not fewer, requirements) as the other students majoring in that discipline.

The tripartite structure of teacher education (foundations, educational psychology, and methods) is not a unified structure; the faculty in each of those areas is very different in educational background, experience, and worldview. Add to the mix the liberal arts and sciences faculty who teach the general education requirements and teach the courses in the major, and the prospective teacher finds herself in an intellectual and ideological maelstrom. In the end, this maelstrom comprises (and *maybe* produces), along with the apprenticeship experience, the "pedagogical content knowledge" of the new teacher.

One way to understand how the teacher education curriculum developed, and why it continues in the present form, is to draw an analogy to the development of the comprehensive school curriculum during the first half of the 20th century. Herbert Kliebard's *The Struggle for the American Curriculum: 1893–1958,* (2004), an examination of the social and intellectual movements that drove the development of the school curriculum in the first half of the 20th century, provides an intriguing answer to the self-contradictory curriculum quandary and its origins. He investigates four major overlapping and layered social and political movements of the first half of the 20th century that shaped what came to be the common school curriculum.

Indeed, most current "reform" proposals are simply rehashes of the four categories, though these categories have become increasingly intertwined and slippery in the years since. Kliebard's book is highly recommended as a heuristic to sort out perspectives and key personalities who have shaped the foundations of U.S. public schooling. In many ways, Kliebard is digging up the tell of the Progressive Era U.S. curriculum in his overview and analysis. He finds each of the layers mixed in with the others and demonstrates that the first sixty-five formative years of liberal progressive school politics were not simple or unified. Certainly, public schooling in the U.S. was not a homogeneous enterprise under the dictatorship of John Dewey. There was no "liberal conspiracy" to simply dismiss.

After analyzing the history of U.S. school policy, Kliebard argues that the successive major social forces that shaped the U.S. curriculum, which he labels humanism, developmentalism, social efficiency, and social meliorism, were simply layered over one another. This layering occurred despite the fact that the ideas were competing with one another, and each was intended to replace the previous idea. As a result, the humanist curriculum remains alongside its proposed replacement—developmentalism. In other words, content and process, frequently proposed as alternatives to each other, were welded together. Social control and social meliorism were layered over the first two in the 1930s and 1940s, despite the fact that each was politically, socially, culturally, and intellectually promoted in opposition to each other. Teachers were faced back then, as they are now, with contradictory and often competing practices, contents, and ideologies in schools, all of which needed to be addressed *consistently* by them in classroom practice and curricular content.

Recurring reconsiderations of the school curriculum and the teacher's role dominate the 20th century and appear to have intensified in the past three decades. These disputes are important to teachers for many reasons, mostly because curriculum affects as well as reflects pedagogy. So it is with the teacher education knowledge base, especially as represented currently by the teacher preparation curriculum. Traditional teacher preparation attempts a mash-up of all these points of view, not always to unified effect. Foundations, educational psychology, and "methods" (i.e., teaching age-appropriate content) are each representative of different worldviews about teaching. Each has its separate piece of teacher education. The historical and cultural development of these conflicting views of the teacher's role remains a central feature of teacher certification, though everyone appears to go to great lengths to make it appear a unified and rationalized system.

The professional preparation program in the education of K-12 teachers encompasses three categories of knowledge. The first part, educational foundations, seeks to teach the intellectual foundations of education in Western society, mostly focused on philosophical and historical writings. The foundations approach, a liberal arts model, emphasizes educational questions and various philosophical teaching traditions (such as the **Socratic method**). However, what teachers learn experientially about *teaching* from the liberal arts and the educational foundations is craft knowledge, since it tends to be about teaching adults. Very little attention is paid to the job of teaching kids; foundations professors, who do not spend much time in schools, not infrequently represent themselves as liberal arts faculty "trapped" in the school of education.

Socratic method

A philosophical inquiry technique named after the ancient Greek philosopher Socrates.

Actual liberal arts faculty who populate the "academic" departments also spend little or no time on pedagogical questions. Nonetheless, many educational foundations courses have been shifted to under-enrolled philosophy and history courses in the liberal arts departments. The alternate response, replacing foundations courses with more "contemporary issues" and "introduction to teaching" courses, can also be found within the colleges of education that are large and powerful. Here is another case where the "solutions" are at opposite extremes of the continuum; in this case, moved either to strictly liberal arts study or to strictly educational study. The current trend toward "introductory" courses is also a rehash of the 1960s move toward more "relevant" foundations requirements. The contemporary practices emphasis may also reflect the paucity of experienced teachers available to oversee apprenticeships or simply reflect the current cultural zeitgeist promoting "change" for the sake of change.

The second part of teacher education, educational psychology, accommodates the scientific model of pedagogical study, most notably through courses in human growth and development and courses in theories of learning. These courses, despite their prior knowledge rationale regarding the requirements of teacher knowledge, tend to emphasize knowledge extraneous to the specific task of teaching kids in school. Instead, educational psychology provides future teachers with knowledge gleaned from over a hundred years of scientific research on human development and learning. Focus on studies of learning, both human and animal, is presented with the idea, as discussed previously, that it is the personal responsibility of the individual teacher to connect these principles of learning to the craft knowledge in the classroom.

The third part of formal teacher preparation and certification is the so-called methods course, so named because it has traditionally focused on teaching "methods," that is, teaching practice. Some professional education course work aims to teach "general methods," that is, how to manage classrooms, how to write a lesson plan, how to keep a grade book, and other elements of the day-to-day life of teachers, but most professional education courses in this new era are "domain specific," given the pedagogical content knowledge emphasis (Stodolsky, 1988).

These teaching methods courses are situated at the place where all of the prospective teacher's formal education is supposed to be synthesized into pedagogical content knowledge, along with experiential learning in classroom apprenticeships usually attached to the course. Methods courses are normally prerequisite to student teaching assignments and are directed and coordinated by the methods instructors. The transformation of "methods" from craft knowledge to professional knowledge came about through the development of articulated pedagogical content knowledge in these courses.

The teaching apprenticeship is ideally part of teacher preparation requirements, but the duration and supervision of the apprenticeship is generally dictated by economic concerns. Increasingly, especially in urban centers with notable teacher shortages and low teacher retention rates, the apprenticeship is done "on the job." Students who originate in lower SES groups see this as a benefit, since it requires less tuition and puts them on the job faster (time is money in this case). Almost ironically, many big cities still require their police and fire professionals to attend "academies" in preparation for becoming professionals and put them in six-month apprenticeships, but no longer see such a system as valuable for new school teachers.

In New York City, the schools chancellor (a lawyer) and the mayor (an information services multibillionaire CEO) have convinced the state to allow most new teachers to be certified with no apprenticeship at all. The head of the teachers' union (a lawyer) has agreed to this arrangement, as have the state legislators (who are generally businessmen and lawyers). On the other side of the coin, more recent efforts by the City University of New York emphasizes more practical experience for prospective teachers beginning as early as the freshmen year of college. Again, here are extremes in the assumptions about the relationship of apprenticeship to certification and to teaching excellence.

Student teaching for a semester with an experienced teacher and a college supervisor has been shown to have a beneficial effect on new teachers' success rates. Most student teaching or apprenticeship assignments provide some lower-risk or, at least, scaffolded or structured on-the-job training. Experienced teachers, some working closely with university teacher preparation programs, and others charting their own courses, enable novice teachers to begin the process of becoming classroom experts through mostly focusing on craft knowledge derived from years of experience.

Even this relatively supportive arrangement, at least in comparison to the on-the-job model, tends to focus almost exclusively on craft knowledge. Craft knowledge for novice teachers, unfortunately, tends to focus on "survival" skills (e.g., "Don't smile until Christmas"), because it assumes a problem-solving orientation ("How do I get the kids to settle down?"). However, if properly addressed by experienced teaching professionals, craft knowledge can result in various refinements of teaching and curriculum and serve as useful scaffolding for learning to teach on one's own over the next few years (given the lack of induction support for new teachers in schools).

Finally, mandated and specified requirements attach themselves to teacher preparation and development during times of "crisis" declared by government authorities. Since the 1960s, reading had been an area of interest, with a concern that every teacher be a teacher of reading. That has now broadened to literacy, with the idea that every teacher should teach reading, writing, and English as a Second Language simultaneously with teaching the content of his/her discipline. Recently, the movement away from segregating special education (developmental disabilities) students has led to requirements for learning about "inclusion" in regular education classrooms. All of these "crisis" requirements are added to the larger course work with the assumption that information and skill are not being dealt with in the existing teacher preparation courses.

Sometimes government policies can be limiting; the policies can even be anti-pedagogy. In the 1980s, Texas legislated to limit the number of credits that could be offered in education for teacher certification programs at the state colleges to a maximum of 18 (Olson, 1989). The rationale was the urban myth that students "were majoring in education instead of a subject matter field." One wonders how the normally minimal 24 credits in education (out of 120 credits at the undergraduate level) for secondary school teachers could be perceived as a "major" in the first place, or how elementary school teachers could teach all the subjects required of them with only six college courses to do the job. It seems clear that part of the problem in taking teaching seriously in recent years is that some governors and legislators and mayors and presidents do not appear to take teachers or teacher knowledge very seriously.

All of these requirements and experiences make up pedagogical content knowledge. Lack of any of those components in teacher knowledge leads to either confused or inappropriate expectations of student performance, students' limited or mistaken understanding of the subject matter, or limited or no learning because of the teacher's lack of skill in managing the classroom learning environment. The formal preparation of teaching professionals at least recognizes the actual complexity of the job set before the novice.

Unfortunately, and unlikely as it seems, this professional model is completely missing from most elementary and secondary schools in which teachers end up teaching. The missing link in most teacher preparation is the "induction" element in the teacher's initial years in the classroom. The missing induction process, something Shulman and his colleagues also cite as the missing link in the development of school professionals, may account for most of the 50 percent dropout rate in the first three years of teaching.

The Tyler Rationale

Whatever the nature and quality of the education of new teachers, or the preference of expert teachers, most curriculum planning in the U.S. continues to be driven by a model known as the Tyler Rationale, based on Ralph Tyler's (1902–1994) comprehensive summary of Progressive Era educational reform and philosophy (and praxis) in his *Basic Principles of Curriculum and Instruction* (1949). Tyler codified the Objectives (Aims), Materials, Methods, and Evaluation approach to school planning that developed during the Progressive Era. Tyler was most interested in classroom practice from a learning, rather than teaching, standpoint, and generally avoided the content of the curriculum question entirely by saying content selection was a matter of using a "philosophical screen." Here is an example of what neoconservatives are attacking when they say that liberal progressive pedagogy ignores cultural content in favor of cultural context and teaching *method*.

The original set of questions that Tyler proposed to drive curriculum and planning were:

- What purposes should the school seek to attain?
- How can learning experiences be selected to help attain these?
- How can learning experiences be organized for effective instruction?
- How can learning experiences be evaluated? (*Basic Principles of Curriculum and Instruction,* 1949)

These were rationalized informally into the aims, materials, methods, and evaluation format, but one can see the original emphasis on learning "experiences" rather than a "content" orientation. Tyler's and others' "philosophical screen" was normally characterized as "democratic schooling."

Not coincidentally, given its abstraction, the "Tyler Rationale" is at the center of the current testing mania generally promoted by both neoconservative and neoliberal education policies. Most of the arguments put forward for "accountability" are based on a "value added" rationale that requires frequent feedback and regular testing to "prove" kids are learning. From either side of the spectrum, the push for evaluation, tied to accountability, appears paramount. The Tyler rationale is the model for doing that sort of curriculum and testing. In fact, the Tyler "philosophical" screen could be put to use as easily by the neoconservative as by the neoliberal: the cultural literacy and core knowledge ideas of neoconservatism are clearly a result of a "philosophical screen."

Despite the various testing frameworks and emerging political positions, curricular discussion of the past century contains a set of assumptions about both *scope* and *sequence* as well as the education of the "whole" child, which normally contains the following structure:

- Cognitive: mental skills (*Knowledge*)
- Affective: growth in feelings or emotional areas (*Attitude or Disposition*)
- Psychomotor: manual or physical skills (*Skills*)

All complete curricula account for each of those categories, and no teacher can afford to neglect any of the above in the classroom (any more than a parent can).

And, yet, current curricular and pedagogical policies appear to focus only on the first and third categories. The whole child is pushed aside. The "affective" domain remains a subject of controversy, except the generally agreed upon notion that students should have the right "attitude" in school behavior. Everyone also appears to agree that teachers need to teach standards of conduct and encourage the humanization of their students, but *how* to accomplish this remains contentious. This problem applies to expectations for teacher *conduct* as well. Recently, in a controversy over something termed teacher "dispositions," its use in certifying new teachers has been questioned. The controversy mimics the cultural war's other battles: are teacher dispositions another way of teaching liberal values to teachers and, worse, denying teaching licenses to those who hold more conservative views? One could say that from the perspective of teacher "attitudes" there is no question that a teacher disposition would be developmental in orientation, intellectually liberal, culturally pluralistic, and committed to the unlimited potential of student learning.

Interesting, Benjamin Bloom, of the Bloom's Taxonomy fame, thought the concept, that is, the *affective,* sufficiently important that he produced a parallel taxonomy for the affective domain in addition to his more famous cognitive domain taxonomy (Krathwohl & Bloom, 1964). What some scholars think is more critical is that he separated the cognitive from the affective. However, experience tells us that defining the "affective" is the only way to guarantee it a curriculum consideration. And still, Bloom's taxonomy of cognitive objectives is all that most curricula employ anyway. **De facto**, the affective is not part of the official formal curriculum. However, it remains part of the "hidden" curriculum of every school, and part of every teacher's classroom practice.

De facto
Doing something as if it were required or expected, without any formal obligation.

Effective Instruction

There were also attempts in the past several decades to synthesize all of the educational research to ascertain whether there were any consistent findings and, therefore, any possibilities for a "what works" compendium for teachers. In an attempt to refine the constant quibbling about "good" teaching, concerted research efforts were expended in the 1970s to determine "effective instructional techniques," which then took on life as "effective teaching." The basic premise was to study teachers who consistently produced (comparatively) high student academic achievement and to see if those teachers possessed any common traits (*traits* is another favorite word in this sort of research).

Effective teaching research seemed to point to several traits of successful academically based learning strategies. Levin, et al., some of the more influential researchers, summarized the work in *Effective Instruction* (1981), suggesting there were three teacher-determined variables that appeared to engender successful long-term learning by students:

1. Active learning time
2. Feedback and corrective measures
3. Instructional cues

Note that the book's title, *Effective Instruction,* with its use of "instruction" rather than "teaching," places the work within the scientific camp of learning research.

The first teaching/learning variable represents the widely employed "time on task" criterion. The more time students spend in active learning, the better they learn. But, the difference in effective classrooms is that students spend significantly more time "actively" engaged in learning. "Actively" is a complicated concept but can be defined or at least distinguished from passive learning. Time on task relates to the active engagement of pupils in learning and means many different things to most policy-makers and teachers. To some it means a longer school day or more homework, to others it means better-designed activities and experiences. It also ties in rather well with Dewey's criterion of "interest"; students will engage more deeply and more often in a task that meets their interests. "Interest" too is a complicated pedagogical concept; it means not only that the student is interested in the topic, but also that it serves the student's interests, including the hope that "If I do well in this algebra course, I can get into a good college."

Feedback
The passing of output back into a system to control its stability.

The second variable, "**feedback** and corrective measures," is the one cited most in the current testing mania. The research is really about both formative and summative evaluation, and the importance of teachers engaging their students in academic discourse, but some have taken it to mean that everything must be "tested." There have been extremes: studies of the University of Chicago-sponsored mastery learning approach to reading found that students were not learning to read in any improved manner, among other reasons, because they were so busy taking tests to receive feedback they had little time to actually read (Goodman, 1985). The emphasis on testing their comprehension took away time for the experience of reading, in a clear case where experience does add up to success.

The question of "feedback," a machine metaphor from stimulus-response behaviorism and cybernetics, makes many teachers of a humanistic bent nervous to begin with. But it is clear that learning is improved if the learner has some sense of how he or she is doing relative to the standard that has been set for achievement. Also, learning is incremental, and more complex tasks and more intricate knowledge need some interim steps.

The third trait of effective teaching is "instructional cuing." This variable is the most dependent on pedagogical practice and craft knowledge. The word "cue" is defined as in a theatrical cue, a signal or a sign to guide the actor. Instructional cuing includes providing or activating students' prior knowledge, making the academic task clear, providing cognitive scaffolding for the knowledge to be learned, and setting clear expectations for the result of the lesson. Note two things for the moment: instructional cuing is a much larger pedagogical category than the other two. Secondly, please note that "setting clear expectations" is not the same as the cry for "setting high expectations" normally heard from school critics worried about "dumbing down" the curriculum. In the end, instructional cuing remains the result of an experienced teacher's codification of classroom conduct and performance.

Process and Product

At the heart of the recent culture wars, as reflected in books about schooling, is a re-ignition of the process versus product debate, sometimes referred to as "process versus content," especially these days when content is such an important marker. Given all the richness and complexity of any of the structures cited above for developing curriculum and teaching strategies, arguments over teaching emphasis and structure are usually reduced to one or two simple orientations. Even in regular professional discourse, the basic orientations of teaching are usually described in terms of one of two primary views of its nature. Teaching, so the proponents of each approach assert, is either:

1. Process-oriented, student-centered, and responding to experience by construction of pragmatic knowledge,

or

2. Product-oriented, subject-centered, and dedicated to the formal acquisition of knowledge.

It does no good to state the obvious, that teaching requires a balance of both approaches for educational and social reasons. The basic ideological debates are fundamentally about process versus product (the student and the text, child and the curriculum, the learner and the discipline). Nothing could be a bigger waste of time than to argue the extremes here, and yet most popular debates underscore the incompatibility of these two views and the superiority of one over the other. In college classrooms, one hears another version of the argument in the ideological distinctions between "quantitative" and "qualitative" research.

The split between student-centered and text-centered originates in the scholarly research areas in universities where teachers are educated. For example, there is a children's literature interest group of the Modern Language Association (the main association for college professors of English and other languages) that focuses almost exclusively on children's literature as "text." They have almost nothing to do with the equally sophisticated group associated with the National Council of Teachers of English that studies children's literature from a student-centered perspective (NCTE is the association of elementary and secondary school English and reading teachers; it also encompasses education professors whose specialty is English or elementary language arts, and many college professors of composition).

Further, there are those interested in children's literature who see themselves as reading or literacy teachers who are not interested in the "canon" of literature for children, but only in children's literature as one more form of text for children to read. Many of those reading teachers and scholars are associated with the International Reading Association, representing the "scientific" study of reading, which distinguishes it in worldview from both the text- and student-centered humanistic approaches. So, within the scientific/humanistic split, we also have the student-centered to text-centered continuum. I emphasize the continuum notion here because scholars range all along this continuum. Unfortunately, these various groups mentioned above tend to cluster together to the exclusion of the "other."

Equally dispiriting in the English curriculum is that groups interested in reading and writing are separated, when it is hardly possible to imagine one as an educational topic without the other. Indeed, most studies show that not only are orality and literacy reciprocal functions, but so are the functions within each: speaking and listening are reciprocal; reading and writing are reciprocal. Further, when one moves to multimodal learning research, one begins to see relationships among the various multiple intelligences (to cite Gardner's categories) or ways of knowing (to cite Eisner's). In other words, even though we might be strongest in visual processing, it has a relationship to our verbal processing. Except possibly in the cases of savants and prodigies, all of our various capacities appear to reinforce one another.

And yet most of our current policy debates fall along these simple divisive lines. The highly politicized debate between "whole language" and "phonics" is a process versus product debate, as is the argument across the schism between quantitative reasoning and formal mathematics. Classroom activities versus lecture, criterion-referenced versus norm-referenced testing, growth orientation versus benchmarks, et cetera, are all process versus product debates.

In the English curriculum, for example, this argument plays itself out in the reading skills versus cultural heritage debate, the process writing versus modes of discourse debate, and the writing and reading versus grammar knowledge debate, among other less important process versus product distinctions. Another example is the "social studies versus history" fight, which is much more than a disagreement over labels. In the school curriculum, conservatives demand a focus on history, especially reading and studying original historical texts. Social studies originates from the liberal progressive movement and reflects the methodology of the social sciences as an approach to teaching and learning.

Mathematics and science are less affected by the naming crisis, but they have their own political wars over process versus product curriculum. There are new disagreements over the sequence in which students take various sciences in the high school, some now arguing that physics should be first in the sequence rather than at the end. There is a continuing debate over so-called sequential mathematics, teaching students age-appropriate combinations of all the different disciplines at each grade level rather than one discipline per grade level. Over the past twenty years, the National Council of Teachers of Mathematics has reversed itself twice on its recommendations for the mathematics curriculum.

As previously referenced, the origin of the "process versus product" curriculum conflict is John Dewey's notion of "psychologizing" the curriculum that was first articulated in *The Child and the Curriculum* (1902) and further refined into the concept of psychological and logical conceptions of the curriculum in *How We Think* (1910). Dewey's argument, in a nutshell, is that the logical organization of the curriculum is based on an adult (i.e., mature) organization of knowledge, while the psychological organization of the curriculum is one that is designed and selected to meet the age-appropriate needs of the learner.

Dewey never argued that one should sacrifice "content" for "process." Rather, the psychological organization of the curriculum, the process approach, is simply a developmentally better approach to achieving the same goal than simply telling the students about the information in a logical manner. The two views of the curriculum are not at odds, in Dewey's view, because the psychologically organized curriculum has as its end goal the logically organized curriculum. The one is the means to the ends of the other, though the psychologized curriculum should have immediate value for the learner, and not be seen as a case of delayed gratification.

Despite the actual reasoning behind the distinction, the exclusionary tension between "content" views and "process" views of teaching any curriculum is not likely to disappear. In any case, the acknowledgment of the interchange between the two opposing views of curriculum actually allows for a dynamic dialogue rather than a dispute between exclusionary camps—and, not to forget the *affective* domain, final choices are always a matter of values. There is the unified vision of Shulman's pedagogical content knowledge model of teacher thinking, and its great potential for changing professional and political discourse.

Finally, there is a "teacher-centered" label (versus "student-centered") that is nothing more than a red herring: all curriculum development is "teacher-generated" (perhaps a better term than "teacher-centered"). Learning might be student-generated, but the curriculum still belongs to the teacher, even within the recent "co-teaching" pedagogies. The teacher is the adult paid to create a learning environment for learners, regardless of the activity base or outcomes. Even a free, humane, sensitive, constructivist classroom is so because the teacher decided that that would be the case. The idea that students might participate in designing the curriculum is a common wish by some, but student participation is always within the parameters set by the culture, the school, and the teacher.

There are as many unanswered questions about curriculum and planning as there are political or cultural or intellectual positions. In the end, the curriculum, even when rendered simply as the "content," can never be established as a static and unchanging set of enduring principles and perennial knowledge, because knowledge is always in cultural flux, both epistemologically and politically. Even the bastions of knowledge—the colleges and universities—exhibit internecine warfare within their walls. There is no place for knowledge to rest and lay its head in peace. There is likewise no intellectual rest for the teacher who must steer the ship of knowledge in the eye of the eternal cultural storm.

Glossary

De facto—A Latin expression meaning doing something as if it were required or expected, without any formal authorization or legal obligation. Contrasted with "de jure," another Latin expression meaning that the practice is sanctioned or determined by law or formal governance.

Feedback—Originally a term from electrical circuit experiments in communications theory, feedback now is widely used in many fields to refer to the passing of output back into a system to control its stability. In learning contexts, that means that student performance is assessed and communicated back to the student to improve the quality of the learning. Within classrooms, feedback is associated with the broader concept of "instructional cuing" in which teachers communicate expectations "on the fly" to students regarding conduct and performance. Feedback was the defining construct in Norbert Wiener's development of the theory of cybernetics, that is, artificial intelligence (AI).

NCATE—National Council for the Accreditation of Teacher Education, an accrediting agency for schools, colleges, and departments of education (SCDE). Founded in 1954 by various educational organizations to oversee and certify high-quality teacher preparation programs.

Novice/expert—Distinction in professional study between inexperienced and experienced practitioners. Research in this area involves the study of the characteristics of novices and experts, and educational practice that moves the professional from one state to the next. Also refers to various studies of apprenticeship in which novices move from "legitimate peripheral participation" to full group membership.

Socratic method—A philosophical inquiry technique named after the ancient Greek philosopher Socrates. As portrayed in the dialogues of his student Plato, Socratic technique uses questioning to reformulate premises and requires the questioner to rethink his own reasoning. The Socratic method is the high point of traditional humanist pedagogy, and the source of the obsession with questions in modern classrooms.

Ways of knowing—An approach to knowledge that emphasizes forms of representation and cognitive processes over knowledge acquisition and recall. Ways of knowing include, for example, quantitative reasoning, aesthetic response to literature, and historiography.

Well-qualified teacher—A set of standards for teacher preparation set by the federal government under NCLB that state schools must meet to continue to receive federal funding. Most specific well-qualified teacher standards are set by the individual states. See http://www.ed.gov/teachers/nclbguide/toolkit_pg10.html

CHAPTER FOUR

Scholarly Disciplines and Content: Teaching Aims and Sources of Knowledge

Another interesting conundrum for pedagogical definition lies in the difference in structure and content between the undergraduate college curriculum and elementary and secondary school courses. Recent demands that schooling be more academic, which normally means more like college teaching, produce sundry dilemmas for content selection. There are contradictions here as well, since it was the college elective model that schools adopted in the 1960s and 1970s that was then later criticized as a "smorgasbord or cafeteria-style" curriculum (Cheney, 1989). Colleges themselves do not have core curricula, though some have gone back to pursuing core knowledge requirements that can be accommodated in various individualized ways.

College curriculum is misaligned with the less complex school curriculum. While the sciences and mathematics in schools are taught as discrete disciplines (except in the sequential math curricula), the social studies curriculum is required to account for all the social sciences plus history. English ends up taking care of literature, cultural studies, rhetoric, art history, and, many times, psychology. That is why any given high school can have an English curriculum that is widely varying in coverage and approach.

There are historical reasons for the mismatch: for one thing, the school curriculum has barely changed over the years while the university curriculum has changed dramatically. The subject called Social Studies came about in the progressive years at the beginning of the 20th century promoted as a reflection of the importance of the new social sciences at the university. In any Progressive Era, history becomes less important culturally, but rather than create a new school subject for sociology and anthropology and the other social sciences, all were collected together under social studies. If one considers the fundamental differences between the traditional *humanistic* rationale for history and the historically recent discipline of political *science*, for example, the possibilities for conflicting philosophies, theories, techniques, and even means of representation should be obvious. To argue that the social studies subject category is a meaningless discipline is only to acknowledge that it is a collision of conflicting knowledge and ideologies.

The situation that social studies teachers find themselves in is repeated in English classrooms, where the subject can be called English Language Arts, or just Reading or Literacy. The debate over "What is English?" is a perennial one, and the problem extends to colleges as well (Scholes, 1999). Certainly, one of the reasons for the problems with English curricula in the schools is that all of the social sciences and humanities that are not included in the formal specified curriculum tend to end up in the English classroom. Some English classrooms operate more like philosophy classes, and some operate as if they were an introductory psychology course. If there were required philosophy and psychology courses in high schools (and why aren't there? you might rightfully ask), then English would not have such an identity problem. English teachers rarely get fired for teaching psychology, especially if it concerns Hamlet's melancholy, or for teaching philosophy if it concerns universal human values.

Science and mathematics each has its own required courses in school curricula: there is biology, chemistry, geology (environmental sciences), and physics along with algebra, trigonometry, geometry, and calculus. Recent attempts at changing that curriculum to sequential mathematics, in which each of the mathematical disciplines are taught in an interdisciplinary manner at each of the high school grade levels, has met with much resistance from college mathematics professors. Also, one would think that the science majors who become science teachers would have the least amount of cognitive dissonance in preparing to be teachers given that *science* undergirds all their training and education. But then one realizes that the behavioral science paradigm and the physical and biological sciences paradigms are at odds with one another, since the first focuses on "human interaction" and the sciences in general focus on studying "nature."

In most cases, science and mathematics education tend toward the formal categorization of knowledge and both use a formal learning model. Students learn science defined as a set of knowledge and procedures, and a worldview based on empirical materialism. They also learn the scientific method, an ideology that encompasses skepticism, materialism, objectification of nature and humans, and a system of proof that relies heavily on replication of results. Contrast that with a notion of teaching based on a humanistic search for eternal verities found in many classrooms and you see where the science teacher might find herself on hostile ground. Science teachers will claim that they teach the "scientific method" and use laboratory experiences to teach it, but nothing about the science curriculum looks like something out of the Progressive Era that spawned it as a school subject in the first place.

Science teachers face the same issues as other disciplinary teachers when it comes to the central conundrum of modern teaching, the war between "subject-centered" teacher and "student-centered" pedagogy. Science and mathematics teachers are rarely on the "student-centered" side of the argument, with even the National Council of Teachers of Mathematics, the most liberal of mathematics teacher groups, presenting the first content standards-based curriculum during the recent neoconservative reform period. Strangely, given their mostly radical worldview—that is, empirical materialism—scientists tend to be pedagogically conservative, mainly because of a belief that there is significant prerequisite knowledge necessary to pursue scientific studies and a rigor necessary to scientific method.

Domain-Specific Knowledge and Interdisciplinary Curriculum

It has become fashionable in some academic and political circles to suggest that disciplinary boundaries are mere administrative conveniences. Critics of traditional disciplines frequently employ that argument to promote their own form of "interdisciplinary" study. And, while it is true that most teachers draw on other **domains** as a means to understanding and teaching their own, only someone who is actually teaching philosophy in place of history, or psychology in place of social studies, or religion in place of mathematics, would say that the disciplinary designation is irrelevant.

Domain
Definition of an academic discipline that includes cognitive processes, cultural expectations, and forms of representation.

Academic disciplines represent culturally approved forms of knowledge. They change with the culture, a recent example being the development of cognitive science departments in colleges, outmoding and absorbing many philosophy and linguistics departments. The redistribution of content from one discipline to another represents a point of view about the nature of the content. In the case of linguistics and philosophy, the two disciplines actually abandoned their humanistic elements and became part of a new science. The only important humanistic function exhibited in philosophy in recent years has been within medical ethics (bioethics) in conjunction with the scientific field of genetics.

Other fields have been transformed or rendered as irrelevant. Speech departments disappeared, as they became departments of communication or media arts and sciences. The Bible became part of the literature curriculum as religious studies moved out of its central role in 19th-century colleges; even today, the argument for the inclusion of the Bible in the public school curriculum is rationalized on the basis of the Bible's literary merit (Reza, 2004). Latin and the classics became mere remnant features of the college curriculum. Shifting domains also reflect the stature of thinking modes as well as relevant content. For example, scholars are now less likely to be "theorists" than to be represented as constructing **data-driven** research models.

Data-driven
In education, a decision-making process utilizing student data on academic performance, attendance, or other countable criteria, to evaluate students and teachers.

Disciplines and scholarly domains themselves can also be constructed as a variation on Elliot Eisner's notion of "forms of representation," or in a conceptual frame that has been termed ways of knowing. In some ways, the "ways of knowing" vision is a process version of the disciplinary model. Ways of knowing is more interested in the psychological and cultural representation of knowledge—what it means to think in that worldview—rather than in focusing exclusively on acquisition of content knowledge.

Ways of knowing could be seen not only as an attempt to bring Dewey's concept of the psychologized curriculum to the academic workplace, but also as a cultural studies approach to knowledge as problematized, socially constructed, and, in the words of European phenomenologists, "interested."

Support for domain-specific knowledge as ways of knowing arrives from both ends of the scholarly spectrum, ranging from the aesthetic connoisseurship of Elliot Eisner (1979) to the cognitive science of Howard Gardner (1982; 1993). In some ways, the best manner in which to talk about interdisciplinary study is illustrated in the Elliot Eisner-edited NSSE collection on *Learning and Teaching the Ways of Knowing* (1985). Structuring the curriculum as *ways of knowing* requires the description of culturally useful knowledge in terms of forms of representation and does so by focusing on the cognitive elements in those domains of understanding. The approach allows for a broader, though more realistic, division of knowledge, skill, and values. Howard Gardner's relatively well-known theory of **multiple intelligences** promotes the ways of knowing argument as well, though he places the sources of the interdisciplinary in the brain of the learner (*Frames of Mind,* 1993).

Multiple intelligences
A theory that human cognition is not unified in a single entity called intelligence.

Domains are ways of accounting for the coverage and organization of knowledge. They can also be liberating in that they allow for attention to new ways of thinking, while maintaining some structure within which the new forms of knowledge can develop. Studies of creative thinking indicate that structure can assist creativity in ways that a lack of guidelines actually discourages. Disciplines can act as **enabling constraints**—cognitive scaffolding that promotes innovation while encouraging reliability within group responses.

Enabling constraint
A structure or limiting framework that promotes creativity and problem solving.

The enabling constraint concept as used by psychologists refers to providing structure for a learning experience. In the teaching of writing it could be specifying the "primary traits" of the discourse. In most classroom instruction, it might be providing specific prior knowledge before an assignment. But enabling constraint is a larger pedagogical notion when seen as a worldview. One recent important use of the enabling constraint concept in political life is the conflict between the liberal and "strict constructionist" views of the U.S. Constitution. The strict constructionists view the Constitution as a sacred document, a complete text that embodies the original and authoritative intent of "The Framers" (formerly the Founding Fathers). The liberal view of the Constitution, a view purportedly embodied in the establishment of the Supreme Court and the provision for legislated amendments, sees the original Constitution as an "enabling constraint."

One needs to go a long way to argue that interdisciplinary organization of the curriculum per se (a stance that assumes disciplines, by the way) is intrinsically superior as an educational frame than a single discipline. But, interdisciplinary work can be powerful as a teaching tool. Heidi Hayes Jacobs' work on interdisciplinary understanding, recently extended into curriculum mapping, distinguishes the various categories currently in play as a mechanism for understanding the possibilities of interdisciplinary learning (1989; 1997; 2004). Her arguments for interdisciplinary teaching account for a range of disciplinary organizations, each carefully rationalized. She is also skeptical about some of the interdisciplinary work currently evident in schools.

Central to Hayes' writings is the importance of carefully distinguishing our rhetoric from our operationalized planning when we connect disciplines. She distinguishes between interdisciplinary and cross-disciplinary, for example. Interdisciplinary brings together the insights of more than one domain, respecting the worldview of each and attempting to see connections between them. Cross-disciplinary involves applying the assumptions of one domain to another domain, and not considering the submerged domain's concepts and disciplinary origins. Most teachers unfortunately engage in cross-disciplinary teaching while calling it interdisciplinary. But Hayes does not completely dismiss cross-disciplinary curriculum and method as essentially wrongheaded; in fact, she argues that they are particularly useful in teaching literacy across domains (given the trans-disciplinary functions of literacy).

In every case, interdisciplinary teaching begins with knowing one's discipline. What follows that understanding could be a borrowing from other domains, a reframing in terms of another domain or an interaction with another way of knowing. But, in the final analysis, the person teaching and learning a domain of knowledge defines it. The individual teacher represents the organization of the curriculum in any classroom. The curriculum resides in the teacher. I can be handed a curriculum for teaching mathematics, and maybe even a script for conducting class, but that does not make me a teacher of mathematics. I can understand how young children learn language, but that does not make me an elementary school teacher unless I understand something about teaching young people in a classroom. However, I can teach in interdisciplinary ways if I view the world through an interdisciplinary lens that keeps my discipline in the center of my vision.

The Hidden Curriculum and Intellectual Traditions

Whatever the other considerations in our curricular practice may be, we tend to acquire a range of philosophical stances that guide our teaching. Many times, these ideas are not part of the formal curriculum, but we have actual expectations for our students based on those assumptions. Some call this the "hidden" curriculum, a form of tacit knowledge. The key statement on the hidden curriculum and its influence on teaching structure and curriculum is Michael Apple's chapter "The Hidden Curriculum and the Nature of Conflict," first published in the paradigm-shifting collection *Curriculum Theorizing: The Re-conceptualists* (Pinar, 1975).

Teaching the conflicts
Teaching contested knowledge in a school setting.

Apple's argument was that history in particular was treated as a manifest destiny-governed story of the progress of democracy, instead of highlighting the conflicting visions of our world discarded or defeated (or continuing) along the way to the present. Apple also argued for highlighting the conflicts within the seemingly hegemonic beliefs of the culture (Apple, 2004). Within university-based cultural and humanities studies, Gerald Graff co-opted and popularized this view in his **teaching the conflicts** approach to cultural theory and pedagogy in the humanities (1981). Teaching differing views promoted dialogical thinking, representing a key metaphor of both critical and creative thinking.

Perennialism
An educational approach arguing that teaching should be concerned primarily with universal and eternal questions and principles of human conduct.

So, if some of our ideas about teaching are not conscious or are at least unarticulated, many times we have overarching aims for our teaching that transcend the local issues and the mandated curriculum. The traditional mindset, the *Ur* model, is the moral view. This pedagogical emphasis is organized around moral goals tied to **perennialist** concerns and seeks authority in its connection to universal standards. It is inherently conservative, mainly because it tends toward what feminist cultural theorists call a patriarchal system of thought, both in content (dead white male philosophers and theologians) and form (historically based prescriptions for living the good life). The moral view of curriculum puts a spotlight on teacher "character" and makes the teacher not only a role model but also an exemplar of behavior. This moral role model function also makes teachers subject to all sorts of conflicting expectations.

The moral view has been supplanted historically by the social efficiency view in many cases, despite the rhetoric one might hear about "traditional moral values." The view has produced technical rationality, systems analysis, and expert systems, all of which are part of the rationale for mass public schooling (see Schön, 1983, on technical rationality). Interestingly, this view of the curriculum provided more opportunity for education, since the meritocracy is a modern scientific efficiency notion. Of course, that concept led to the logical conclusion of providing educations for the "workers" different from those for the "managers." The scientific view is utilitarian, emphasizes social control, and puts great faith in the scientific method for discovering truth and in technology for delivering that truth to the people.

This technical-rational model provides the "what works" formula. The curriculum is broken down into discrete skills taught for mastery and assessed and controlled by standardized, "objective" (a word whose implied philosophical meaning carries a stronger meaning than the psychometric technical meaning) testing. The central image of this view is the bell curve, a model in which the vast majority of people are "in the middle," where most of the students are "average" and expectation of average-ness is the "norm."

Social reconstruction
Schools used as a component in building a new social order.

An additional cultural perspective is the social justice or **social reconstruction** argument, traditionally identified with John Dewey and the Progressive Education Association. This curriculum view seeks to change society and sees education as working towards that purpose. Social reconstructionism is very attractive to teachers and professors as it increases their social importance, at least from that perspective. On the other hand, this view can be limiting because it is largely political, regardless of the ideology applied, and does not intend to be inclusive. In recent years, the reverse argument has appeared, that is, schools have no influence on society, and school reform can come only from the outside (see Anyon, e.g.).

A fourth perspective is the grand Romantic tradition, which these days could be called the authentic naturalist cultural theory, because it claims insight into the authentic nature and behavior of humans and is basically anti-urban, anti-politics, and anti-technology. The line here runs from Rousseau to Thoreau, from transcendentalism to New Age thinking. This perspective places most value on the individual and his or her human potential, though it also encompasses psychotherapeutic approaches. Though the emphasis can be on a subject domain, many of the Romantic views of the curriculum teach personal enlightenment or social responsibility as more important than school knowledge. This view emphasizes cultural forms and human expression, promoting growth in a social context normally without deterministic social theories. It seeks to expand human possibility, rather than particularize, determine, socialize, or moralize human behavior and thought.

All of these positions are philosophical positions that may precede but cannot preclude pedagogical issues. Philosophy, even tacitly, may direct us, but each of these positions is insufficient as it stands for teaching. In other words, none of these philosophical positions can substitute for pedagogy, in much the same way that a logical organization of the curriculum is not possible without a means for attaining it educationally. "Believing" something is not the same as "knowing" it, but sometimes belief is all we have to go on. As professionals, we need to remain skeptical about our beliefs, and not merely "passionate" about them. A lot of bad actions in history have been based on belief, from the Inquisition to the Holocaust.

Special note needs to be made of the cultural perspective, since it appears so dominant in our current professional discourse. One of the difficulties of the cultural approach is that the word **culture** has become a slogan. Some people use the term "cultural" interchangeably with "philosophy" and others see everything they do as "cultural." "Cultural" has more of an apolitical meaning than it probably should, but it does seem to denote certain pedagogical tendencies. The cultural perspective, unlike the deterministic stance of the political, or the ideals of the philosophical, promotes dialectical and expansive relationships and tends to celebrate (note the use of "celebrate" as an element of that discourse) the creative over the analytical and "scientific."

Culture
The pattern of beliefs and behaviors and artifacts in human societies.

The cultural looks to the common and the commonplace for clues to learning and tends to exalt human achievement in a culturally pluralistic and egalitarian manner.

Our operational definition of curriculum is usually a mix of the above. Our curriculum and our teaching stance are not unified overall and tend not to be unified even in the individual teacher. If it were unified, it likely would be somewhat limiting both in possibility and appeal to the students. It is precisely this multiple perspective approach that requires clear articulation. However, it is not enough to say: "My curriculum is eclectic," as if that explained anything. The teacher-organized vision of the discipline, the curricular emphasis, and student understanding and performance should all be articulated even as a contingent **rationalization**. In fact, the attempt to find a unitary model for teaching is a remnant of the positivist, scientistic trend in education. Teaching requires a kaleidoscopic model, with reciprocal theories to deal with the dialectical and even dualistic nature of knowledge. A unitary model simply will not suffice, especially when the purpose of finding unity erases both difference and conflict in our thinking.

Rationalization
A constructed logical justification for practices or beliefs or social circumstances.

The language of various intellectual models is important to our understanding and articulation of cultural understanding. The notion of "problem solving" comes from the scientific/technological perspective. Dewey's social reconstructionist perspective would remind us that problem-construction, that is, what problem we choose to solve, is as important as the means of solving the problem. Much of the problem in contemporary educational discourse is that someone is always declaring a crisis and demanding, usually for national security purposes, that we "solve" the "problem." But, problem solving means what it says: it is looking for solutions.

The search for unity is part of our current intellectual paradigm, even outside of science. One of the problems of national school systems in the past century was the establishment of "patriotic" curricula. All teachers in public schooling are part of the citizenship curriculum. It comes in many forms, the most obvious being the flags and Pledges of Allegiance and the focus on U.S. history and good behavior. But it also exists in subtle and submerged forms. The children's literature curriculum has its roots in the collection (and creation) of national myths and fables that became stories of the national character. Almost all children study "mythology" and folklore in elementary school, much of which is purported to provide a "foundation" for reading and for cultural literacy. This content draws from what began as "scientific" investigations of the native culture of the people in the newly formed countries in Europe.

Hans Christian Andersen made nationalistic claims for Denmark against the other Scandinavian countries, while the principalities that became Germany were united by a common German folk culture around myths of Valkyries and heroes that evolved into Wagner operas and national pride and big rallies (you know where that went from there). To this day though, little kids study mythology because of the notion that it is part of the human subconscious, part of our "cultural heritage." American tall tales and folk traditions have been layered over the great folk and fairy tales of Europe.

In the social melioration period of American education, 1947–1958, these books started to show a "psychological orientation": stories as prescriptions for living in which family dramas were played out; or little kids or bunnies found true happiness in the bosoms of their family; or when ugly ducklings found they could grow into beautiful swans. Those who want to include study of mythology from the point of view of psychology, or from the point of view of structuralism or nationalist prior knowledge, are all engaging the same argument. In fact, all we have done lately with the same notion is make it more multicultural by adding fairy tales from other lands to the curriculum (e.g., a Chinese "Cinderella" story). Not very scientific, any more than racial theories based on 19th-century science promoted by this sort of study, and yet we still hold on to the content and the approach without any articulated reason for doing so.

The impulse to provide answers, to be certain, creates havoc with the language of teaching. We simply say we are teaching reading "skills" without any clear sense of what that means. Despite all the research and all the emphasis on reading, we generally have no idea what we are doing except to say we are teaching "critical thinking" and reading "skills." Every reading program is certainly much more than that; to be useful to the students, teachers should have a better grasp of what all of those motives and intentions are (Shannon, 1989). But to say we do not know what we are teaching is unacceptable in public policy.

The quest for unity also tends to leave out the more problematic elements of culture, especially those that promote diversity and creativity rather than problem solving and criticality. The cultural view that is most lacking and the most lamented by key theorists is the **aesthetic** point of view. Suzanne Langer, author of the paradigm-breaking *Philosophy in a New Key*, devotes several books to the subject, the most important entitled *Feeling and Form*. In *Philosophy in a New Key* (note the musical metaphor), Langer is the first philosopher to assert that an intellectual age is not defined by the philosophical answers to eternal questions but by the questions that are asked in the first place. This is parallel with Dewey's notion that the first step in problem solving is deciding on the problem and defining the problem.

Aesthetics
Understanding focused on human representation and holistic thinking in opposition to the fragmentation and reduction of rationalized thinking.

Langer is the source of one of the great observations regarding the school curriculum and the arts. Lamenting that only literature, of all the arts, is in the list of formal academic curriculum requirements, she observes:

> The reason why literature is a standard academic pursuit lies in the very fact that one can treat it as something else than art. (1953, p. 208)

She is referring not only to the tendency of schools to read books only for "information," but also to their penchant for reading literary works as a search for a reduced statement of "what the author is trying to say," normally constructed as a moral statement or "theme," as in, "Greed leads to moral degradation" or "Society can overwhelm the best intentions of even good people." Aesthetic modes of knowing are essential to thinking but are frequently ignored in classrooms and educational research (Eisner, 1985; 1993).

The prolific and influential educational philosopher Maxine Greene has extended Deweyan philosophy into the realm of the aesthetic (1981; 1988; 2000). Greene's argument surrounds the reintegration of the aesthetic into the social fabric, as a necessary part of the democratic structure. For Greene, the arts constitute the democratic element in education, from asking the "what if" question to the form of associative and creative thinking much of the art curriculum pursues. Without art there is no democracy in the classroom, from the aesthetic point of view.

Within the aesthetic view of teaching is a worldview that does not necessarily jibe with the humanistic "content" view of the curriculum. And, the "art of teaching" argument is frequently not an aesthetic argument, but simply an inarticulate rendering of the humanist curriculum argument. There is also an aesthetic argument for teaching purpose and style that has been argued over the years (Rubin, 1985). However, one of the complications of talking about the aesthetics of teaching is the same problem of talking about art with artists: they insist they cannot talk about it, that is, the art speaks for itself. In Albin Zak's *Poetics of Rock*, one of the wisest scholarly books on creativity and music, he provides an analogy from the world of rock music, which he describes as "*mostly* an aesthetic category" [emphasis in origin]:

> rock recordists, though they share musical and technical resources and are influenced by stylistic and commercial guidelines that can be quite specific, stress repeatedly that there are no rules. ... Even working within a conventional system with all sorts of stylistic guidelines and normative procedures, the success of their rhetorical flourishes depends upon creative musical imagination, not logical justification. For though it works within boundaries, the creative musical spirit values the "lucky find" far above the deliberate argument. (2001, p. 189)

If one substitutes *pedagogical* in the above statement for *musical and rhetorical* (Zak's own "language" analogy to bolster his musical description), the basic argument for aesthetic or artistic teaching should be as clear as one can make it. It would be best for all if the artistic teacher could develop an articulated sense of aesthetic educational practice that informs the teaching. In any case, there seems to be at least an internal "logic" to the aesthetic form.

Psychological Theories and Teaching

The other big distinction in these times is between two sorts of approaches to psychological research, specifically research about developmental stage theory and learning theory. Two contemporaries represent the two basic positions: Swiss psychologist Jean Piaget (1896–1980) and Russian psychologist Lev Vygotsky (1896–1934). Piaget is still well known for his developmental theories, focusing on the movement from concrete to abstract thinking and describing analytical and quantitative reasoning abilities in children. Piaget's pioneer work underlies modern cognitivist research. Much of teacher talk in everyday use originated from the Piagetian school, including taxonomies, developmental stages, concrete and abstract thinking, etc.

It was only after the 1960s' translations of Piaget's contemporary Lev Vygotsky's research that a viable alternative theory has been available. Vygotsky's work focuses more on language development and the social nature of learning. Positing the notion of the "zone of proximal development," Vygotsky's research describes one way in which the learner can develop maturity at various stages with the assistance of a "teacher." Vygotsky's work has also promoted the change in focus from "instruction" to "teaching," since it emphasizes the role of the adult (or an expert or simply a more mature or experienced individual) in the learning relationship with children. Modern "cultural psychology," a more humanistic response to behavioral psychology and some forms of cognitivism, derives from the influence of Vygotsky.

Hierarchies define Piagetian models, with the well-known Bloom's Taxonomy being the one most employed in curriculum design and pedagogy. Vygotsky's influence leads some to speak of "webs of meaning" rather than hierarchies, showing ideas in relation to one another rather than as stacked up in levels of importance. This new cultural psychology has much to offer, since it does away with the obsession with "prior knowledge" and "preparation" and paves the way for "situated learning." Leading practitioners of cultural psychology include Silvia Scribner and Michael Cole, but even some of the great stage theory psychologists, such as Jerome Bruner, have moved into a sociohistorical frame of reference for discussions of psychology and learning. Inventor (in 1961) of the "spiral curriculum" that we still see in "innovative" curricular projects, Jerome Bruner also discusses oral transmission of culture and the reasons for the continuation of certain teaching practices in his career-capping *Acts of Meaning* (1990) and *The Culture of Education* (1996).

The distinctions above relate to the psychological research that actually studies humans. Cognitive science theory, research, and computer modeling techniques have grown in influence in recent years and have come to dominate learning theories. Schema and prior knowledge are two of the more influential concepts from cognitive science. But cognitive science, with its reliance on computer modeling and analysis of large data sets, is only part of another revolution, the shift from theoretical to data-driven research.

The most notorious application of the data-driven work is in the use of the Comstat approach to school assessment. Assessment is now driving educational thinking in the United States under the twin banners of accountability (financial and cultural) and scientific management (measuring achievement and adjusting instruction accordingly). Scientific management has been promoted in this country during the 20th century as efficient and even wise. Recent versions of scientific management include the successful Comstat approach to police work that has been credited with the reduction of crime in the country: "Comstat is a collection of modern management principles, military-like deployment efforts and strong enforcement strategies all informed by accurate statistical crime data" (Dussault, 2000). One wonders how such a system could be adapted to teaching children, or why it would be employed in the first place.

In school policy, the "data" is student achievement scores on standardized tests. If the students are not doing well on tests then the focus changes to improving test performance. The improvement, since the materials are standardized, would come in the teaching. Either the teacher would perform "better" or she would be removed or replaced. If the teacher is doing well and the child "refuses" to learn, the student is held back a grade or is provided with additional teaching after school or in the summer until the test is passed. Most of the above looks like a punishment scenario, and one can see the problem of the analogy of teaching with police work.

Though much of the discussion of assessment comes from the educational psychology paradigm, the Comstat approach is an excellent example of one of the new "data-driven" approaches to social policy and social management. These data-driven models have no theoretical frame at all; Comstat can be used only to improve test scores with no sense of the value of the testing, the validity of the tests, or the value of the knowledge "learned," that is, exhibited on the test. To combat this lack of purpose, Grant Wiggins' work on student assessment tries to restore some of the humanistic purposes to the assessment process (1999).

Serious professional discussion of the uses of evaluation for teaching and learning can be found in the National Research Council–sponsored collection, edited by James Pellegrino, in which a distinguished group of evaluation experts proposes a new model for pursuing evaluation in schools, one that accounts for all the stakeholders and includes a range of evaluation as criteria for judgment rather than the reductive attachment to "high stakes" objective testing. Pellegrino and his distinguished colleagues call for a modern reassessment of assessment itself by employing the ample work that has been done since these tests were established and normed: "This body of knowledge strongly implies that assessment practices need to move beyond a focus on component skills and discrete bits of knowledge to encompass the more complex aspects of student achievement" (2001, p. 102).

One reason for the continued commitment to the current evaluation system is that these tests have provided stability. But, in a changing culture these tests also legitimate discrimination. For years, in the past, female students performed significantly worse than male students on standardized tests in mathematics, though the young women received higher school grades. The test results were used to discriminate against young woman seeking careers in science and technology. There was actually an argument that women were "wired differently" from men, an opinion that still exists in some circles (recently, the president of Harvard University lost his job over saying as much). Elizabeth Fennema's careful research had demonstrated no differences in the cognitive structure and academic ability of young woman in mathematics (Fennema & Leder, 1990). The research promoted the idea that female students could, in an atmosphere of new cultural attitudes, succeed in any area as measured by legitimated standardized tests. Over the past several years, women have been scoring as well as men on these tests. That could not have been an evolutionary leap; the earlier perception was simply a matter of prejudice in school. It also shows how cultural attitudes can shape "scientific" testing; one wonders if the so-called performance gap between black and white students might disappear under similar circumstances.

Outside of teaching students the secrets of test-taking behavior, widely available to students whose parents can afford private tutoring at Kaplan or the Princeton Review, much of standardized testing is outside the direct influence of the teacher. Grade reporting, a formal responsibility of teachers, is a different species of judgment. It remains one of the most reliable measures of student achievement as well, even though most teachers would be hard-pressed to articulate exactly how grades are assigned. And, in the end, it is the formative evaluation/assessment, rather than the summative, that is of most interest to the teacher, because formative evaluation is directly aimed at improving learning rather than merely judging it. Most teachers look at the assignment of quarterly grades as formative assessment in any case.

The most recent scholarly trends under the cultural psychology and social learning banner are seen in studies of "situated learning," and with the notion of situated learning comes the epistemological assertion of "situated knowledge." Lave and Wenger's work, originally focusing on apprenticeship and the development of expert knowledge, argues that knowledge is always situated, that knowledge is temporal and always in a cultural context (1991). In other words, we do not "know" something in the sense we have it stored in our brains in some sort of neutral way. We know things only in the context of the situation in which we find ourselves. This insight applies even to school knowledge: we know some things in a certain way for school and another for outside of school. This formulation describes not only most adolescent behavior, but also specialized understanding of adults that varies by situation.

Communities of practice
Groups of people who share a concern or a passion for something they do, and learn how to do it better as they interact regularly.

Wenger's further work postulates **communities of practice**, an efficacious means for learning and doing in cultural contexts (1999). Communities of practice require a social definition of cognition and provide a dynamic vision of the concept of common culture. Communities of practice are another way of addressing the expert pedagogue question, as one moves from legitimate peripheral participation as a novice to community leadership as an expert. And communities of practice, broadly conceived, also address the continuing wrestling match over common culture, even if it is merely the common culture of the community.

This question of the need for a common culture is not a small one. The academic focus of the neoconservative counter-revolution focused on attacking the "smorgasbord" or "cafeteria style" curriculum developed in school during the 1960s and 1970s, suggesting that a common curriculum was necessary for the preservation of the culture (Bloom, 1987; Cheney, 1987). The liberal concern for choice was rationalized as a multicultural curriculum, in opposition to a defined common culture curriculum. But, neoliberalism also looked to regularize the content of the curriculum. Key cultural debates, and subsequent legislation, of schooling in the twentieth century have always revolved around who shall be educated and what the content and nature of that education should be.

For example, requiring four years of English classes, promoting history over social studies, and choosing books written by dead white females all are cultural decisions. The definition of community and the community of practice for teachers are inextricably entangled. Teachers play many roles in the community and, therefore, engage in conflicting communities of practice at any given time. An orthodox believer of any religion who teaches in a public school would be a prime example of someone who would need to balance significantly different roles in two very different communities of practice.

But teachers need to establish some sort of structure in their thinking about classroom teaching and need to address the question of the curriculum-in-action. For a classroom teacher, curriculum is a set of principles, beliefs, guidelines, and knowledge for planning learning experiences and transmitting cultural knowledge. A consistent and comprehensive curriculum should be guided by models of human growth and learning, informed by the current social climate. As a result of the need for comprehensiveness and appropriateness, the guiding principles should be expressed at a general level of learning theory and social aims; the individual particulars of the actual lesson should be selected within local cultural norms. As for the common culture, that changes with the culture. The common culture reflects situated knowledge and can never be put into a perennialist vision of unchanging universal knowledge.

Future Knowledge and Control of the Curriculum

The future is already here. Film is over 100 years old. Radio has been around for generations, and newer wireless technologies have filtered down to elementary school students. Television has saturated our culture in a mere fifty years and now extends its reach through computers and other video sources. The personal computer has transformed learning. Digital sound has made everyone a musician, or at least a record producer. In the future, the years 1450 to 1950, between the invention of the moveable type printing press by Gutenberg and the mass distribution of television, will be known as the Age of Text. We now live in a multimedia universe that requires new literacies.

The computer is already so integral to our learning and doing that we cannot remember what it was like to write before the computer. The personal computer has facilitated process approaches to writing in schools and made it more likely that writing will be revised. Simple artificial intelligence programming helps us spell words and get our tenses right. Combined with the Internet, the personal computer is our typesetter, our reference book, and our personal library of information, easily integrating text, audio, and video.

More importantly, the personal computer, in concert with the Internet, has changed the source, the structure, and the production of knowledge. That is the real revolution in learning that must be accounted for in future pedagogy. Most students prefer word processors not because they can revise their writing, but because they can *publish* it. The reason for the wild popularity of MySpace.com and other personal networking sites lies in the publication and production, even if it is just knowledge about one's self. Students now produce knowledge as much as learn it.

The nature of expertise changes in cyberspace, where bloggers can carry more influence as self-publishers than if they were required to go through more traditional legitimated channels. Wikipedia is an exercise in social networking and distributed processing. The level of expertise represented in Wikipedia is arguably equivalent to any modern encyclopedia. Teacher experts in the future will be teachers who put their knowledge on display on websites and attract a following of other teachers who log on to their site. One's community of practice is no longer limited to either local colleagues or legitimated professional organizations, but to what James Gee calls "affinity spaces." Your colleagues are defined by access to the World Wide Web, and your best partner colleague could be teaching in Sweden or Chile.

What all of this change means for teachers is teaching students how to negotiate new sources of knowledge and new ways to make the process of knowing more visible and more immediate. The Internet reminds all of us that knowledge is a social construct in ways that we have forgotten regarding books and other mass media. I suppose we could easily forget again, but the exponential growth of knowledge and its representation in public spaces has forever changed official knowledge and secret knowledge.

But, not everyone sees open access to knowledge as a common good, and many see control of the Internet as the next step in cultural limitation and restriction. After all, there are those who still believe the calculator is a barrier to mathematical understanding rather than a cybernetic necessity. Much of government policy appears to be about restricting culture rather than expanding it. The first great debates in Congress when any new medium is introduced are hearings on regulation or censorship. This legislative impulse is based on the notion that citizens need to exhibit certain behaviors to be good citizens and that government exists to control natural impulses.

Since schools require the production of citizens for the republic, much of school practice is aimed at appropriate behavior. Teachers do not like to think of themselves as teaching "behavior" instead of knowledge and skills and values, but most of the critics of the school system attribute crime and other deviant behavior to teachers failing to "enforce discipline." Actually, most inexperienced teachers quit or are fired because of classroom discipline problems. But, a disciplined classroom is not an end in itself. However, completing school by negotiating the system is also part and parcel of the "certification" and "credentialing" function of schooling that can expand one's opportunities in the world, and teaching one's students how to navigate that system seems a sensible goal.

The problem here is that we have all sorts of built-in contradictions in the ideologies surrounding the curriculum of control. First, a person's behavior is based on experience, and on cultural and social expectations. One learns how to act through experiencing one's culture. The problem in the U.S. is that schools seem to be trying to turn people from other cultural backgrounds into "Americans," but we do not appear able to define what it is to be an American. We no longer embrace the metaphor of the "melting pot," and we appear to have no interest in internationalism or multiculturalism. There are those who believe that U.S. culture is homogeneous and all new immigrants must conform to an ideal of American culture, and then there are those who argue that the U.S. has always been and will always be a multicultural society and that the society is constantly reconstructing itself as new people arrive, regardless of attempts to freeze the culture.

This is a political debate, but it affects the most basic elements of pedagogy in American schools. For example, unlike most other advanced postindustrial nations, the U.S. has a de facto (and increasingly de jure) policy of monolingualism. Whereas most kids around the world who speak more than one language are considered sophisticated, in the U.S. those who speak a language in addition to English are considered educational "problems" and receive little education in any language other than English—unless they come from the leadership classes and are required to learn a "foreign" language (Osborn, 2002). The argument has been won, for now, by the monolingual advocates; although one finds some instruction in ESL (English as a Second Language), there is little, if any, bilingual education, regardless of the endless rhetoric about a global-based information economy that awaits our graduates.

A third complexity for the pedagogical future is maintaining the focus of the discussion. Even when one eliminates the political, and even social, effects of the schooling argument from the serious discussion of pedagogy, one is left with the eternal triangle of student, teacher, and subject. In the teachers' workroom, one sometimes hears discussion of new teaching approaches or material shut down by someone emotionally invoking the rights and the interests of the students. Other times, teachers may insist that students must simply buckle down and work because the class has "material to cover." And, of course, the class is directed and engaged by the teacher's skill and knowledge, and the professional responsibilities of the teacher. These basic positions on students' rights versus responsibilities, the purpose and role of the teacher, and the commitment to formal knowledge and the cultural imperatives are equally important. To focus on one at the expense of the other may be necessary for specific purposes, but to privilege one over the other demeans the role of the other two.

Articulation is a necessary facet of teacher understanding: we must be able to say what it is we are doing to claim any value for what we do. There is no free lunch with teaching. We owe it to our own development, to our pupils' education, and to the society that employs us to be able to name what we do, articulate our thinking, explain our behavior, and justify (from a range of perspectives) our aims. To do less cheapens the profession. And, in the end, our failure to articulate our own discipline threatens the subject, encouraging outside critics, internal confusion, and cult-like special interest groups. The end of any subject matter discipline comes when even the practitioners refuse to discuss it. How can those outside a discipline value it if the practitioners of the discipline cannot name its value in socially useful terms? Knowledge of this sort is specific and codified, even traditional in some senses. It arises from our collective past mixed with our individuated history; it reflects past interests and perennial hopes. To coin a phrase, curriculum making is defining the discipline. No definition, no domain.

Glossary

Aesthetics—Normally seen as a branch of philosophy concerned with the beautiful and pleasurable, aesthetic modes of understanding are now frequently contrasted with technical rationality to provide an alternative to functionalist thinking. Aesthetic modes of understanding tend to focus on human representation and holistic thinking in opposition to the fragmentation and reduction of rationalized thinking.

Communities of Practice—A concept popularized by Etienne Wenger, communities of practice are, in his words, "groups of people who share a concern or a passion for something they do and learn how to do it better as they interact regularly" <http://www.ewenger.com/>. Communities of practice serve as models for professional activity and classroom teaching. They also serve as models of socially constructed forms of intelligence.

Culture—The pattern of beliefs and behaviors and artifacts in human societies. Modern meanings of culture in educational studies and projects eschew the old distinctions between high and low culture and do not see the end of formal education as being "cultured."

Data-driven—In school policy, a decision-making process utilizing student data on academic performance, attendance, demographics, or other countable criteria, to be used by administrators, teachers, and parents to assess student learning. Derived from computer-based social science research, data-driven policy decisions discard theory for "evidence."

Domain—In curriculum making, a more expansive definition of an academic discipline that includes cognitive processes, cultural expectations, and forms of representation in addition to subject matter content or skills.

Enabling constraint—A useful concept in many fields, a structure or limiting framework that promotes creativity and problem solving. In classrooms, enabling constraints are used by teachers to set expectations for an assignment, including controlling the range or reliability of responses, or providing advance organizers for reading or comprehending.

Multiple intelligences—A theory proposed by Howard Gardner that human cognition is not unified in a single entity called intelligence. Instead, there are various sorts of human intelligences, though different individuals are stronger in one than the others. He named those intelligences: bodily-kinesthetic, interpersonal, verbal-linguistic, logical-mathematical, naturalistic, intrapersonal, spatial, and musical. Gardner argues that school privileges verbal-linguistic intelligence over the others, thus inadequately providing appropriate education for those who are stronger in other areas of intelligence.

Perennialism—An educational approach arguing that teaching should be concerned primarily with universal and eternal questions and principles of human conduct. In the U.S., identified with Robert Maynard Hutchins and Mortimer Adler's Great Books curriculum.

Rationalization—A constructed logical justification for practices or beliefs or social circumstances. Sometimes contrasted with reasoning, rationalization is focused on standardization and sequential or logical ordering. The unitary and sequential organization of teacher preparation programs, and even college majors, is a rationalization.

Social reconstruction—An idea associated with Progressivism; in educational thinking, it means teaching and schooling should be used as a means for building a new social order.

Teaching the conflicts—Also known as teaching the controversies, or differences, an approach to teaching contentious or contested knowledge in a school setting. Ideally, as promulgated by Michael Apple and Gerald Graff, the approach promotes understanding ideas as dynamic, dialogical, and problematic. Politically, the idea has caught on as a means to integrate competing worldviews, such as creationism, into public schools.

CHAPTER FIVE

The Intellectual Teacher: The Epistemology of Pedagogy

The teacher is a professional, but even expert status in that role does not make us infallible. The world is rife with illusion and misunderstanding. Scholarly research itself is predicated on the fact that we do not know enough. Equally, as educated people, we are part of a long series of socially constructed conventions of knowledge. We take for granted all sorts of information and behavior, even if we have no personal rationale for believing or doing certain things. Teachers are required to make knowledge "visible" and to pursue new knowledge and new understandings of what we already know. But, then, how much does anyone really know, even if we can define what it means to *know* something?

We are born into a world we did not make, a world with established ideas and cultural conventions. This primer follows some traditional structures of argument, in the rhetorical and academic sense. These conventions should be transparent since this is a book about pedagogy. Some would argue that all teaching should be transparent, doing away with distinctions between "secret knowledge" and "visible knowledge" (Bass, 2008; Kermode, 1979). Some of that debate concerns the role of the expert, the nature and function of knowledge, and articulated knowledge versus "intuition" or "tacit knowledge." However, in this primer, everything is illuminated—as much as possible, certainly, given the human limitations of knowledge.

So, in traditional western European culture, argument quite often requires a quotation from the ancient Greeks or Romans, followed by a formal definition of the topic. A quote from the ancients follows, along with an illustration of how that mode of argument functions. This will be followed by discussions employing various concepts, analysis, examples, analogies, etc., all part of the teacher's "tool kit." Following this discussion, in the next chapter, there will be discussion of teacher language and the discourse of education, plus the effect of language on teaching and in talking about teaching.

In the interim, simply note that modern philosophical discourse normally includes "linguistic analysis" for clarification of meaning. Linguistic analysis, at least in its informal use, is a habit of mind one learns in undergraduate study in all of the liberal arts and sciences. For example, the use of "tool" in the previous sentence should have raised questions in the reader's mind: what does the author mean by a *tool*? Both a *hammer* and a *computer* are tools (so is a *gun* and a *smile*). Which category of "tool" does the writer mean when he talks about pedagogical tools?

There are all sorts and levels of pedagogical tools. This primer includes wide margins for reader notes and questions, as well as definitions in glossary form. Both wide margins and glossaries are pedagogical tools. Pedagogical tools normally include textbooks and all the apparatus that attends them. Pedagogical tools include normative structures of teaching themselves (introducing the topic, checking homework, etc.), since most have been shown to be viable over the years. Pedagogical tools also include performance variables, including the judicious use of the aforementioned *smile*. In this case, the pedagogical tool is a text used to teach a concept or an idea.

Quotations from the ancient Greeks and Romans, as an element of intellectual discourse, originate in the Reformation/Renaissance (though the ancient Greek and Latin intellectuals liked to cite their colleagues and forebears). With this intellectual convention, the new humanist scholar's thinking could be immediately distinguished from that of a medieval theologian, whose stock in trade were quotations from the Bible. Quoting an

Stance
A psychological term suggesting a predisposition or a point of reference that is intentional and rationalized.

ancient source was a political statement as well as an intellectual **stance** in the Renaissance. This tradition of politicking by source quotation remains alive today in the differences between secular and religious arguments. These rhetorical distinctions have important consequences. For example, a few years ago, one could witness a successful U.S. presidential candidate cultivate evangelical Christian votes by publicly announcing that his favorite philosopher was Jesus.

This intellectual marker remains alive also in the distinctions between scientific and humanistic discourse. The scientific revolution and the dropping of Latin and Greek as the language of instruction in universities have virtually eliminated the use of humanistic quotation in the physical and social sciences discourse. Scientific research does not draw on the wisdom of past generations, but on a history of empirical findings and scientific interpretation. Science writing "quotes" scientists. The humanities normally quote scientists only if the scientists appear to support humanistic positions (Gould, 1996; 2007, e.g.). However, especially in the humanities, one uses the quotation from the ancients (and even modern humanists) for the same reason as in the past: to demonstrate knowledge of and support for the humanistic traditions.

One can easily see how the question of preparation for learning, and the "prior knowledge" element of learning, can be difficult to manage. You are now saying to yourself, when is this author going to get to the ancient Greek quotation he keeps talking about? The balance between *preparation* (a *very* loaded word in pedagogical thinking) and actual learning remains one of the most problematic methodological questions in classrooms. Some teachers, at least it seems that way, spend more time on preparation for learning than on learning experiences themselves. And a favorite topic among college faculty is how "unprepared" their students are, assuming that what these professors are moved to teach is dependent on earlier teachers' efforts rather than their personal responsibility. Having said that and having demonstrated my point about too much preparation and prior knowledge, here comes the quote from the ancients.

Hippocrates, the ancient Greek physician, once wrote, regarding the work of healers, "make a habit of two things — to help, or at least to do no harm" (*Epidemics*, Bk. I, Sect. XI). That statement could be the creed of the teacher as well, which is the point of selecting it for this primer. The first commitment of the teacher is to not harm children (or adolescents and adults). But, of course, even the notion of what is harmful to children is not easily determined. Corporal punishment, that is, spanking, used to be considered "good" for children. "Spare the rod, and spoil the child," as the old proverb goes. Today, corporal punishment is cause for legal action against adults, including parents. Then again, a not so insignificant percentage of children are being drugged for various "behavior problems," "for their own good," or so the saying goes. However, unless one simply wants to argue, one must say that the role of the teacher, *in a democratic society*, is to help children grow, rather than limit their development.

Teachers teach knowledge, but that knowledge is frequently contentious and often inaccurate. The ancient quotation in the above paragraph, for example, is widely thought to reside in the *Hippocratic Oath*, a work commonly referenced in popular culture and sometimes used as a professional oath for physicians. But, the quotation is not in the Hippocratic Oath's text. Hippocrates is believed to have written the words though in another context. Translators have also differed on the translation, and classical scholars have disagreed on its meaning in its historical context. Knowledge, it seems, is not very certain, even the most taken-for-granted knowledge or "common" knowledge.

We are also creatures of rumor, bias, and tall tales. A very influential early U.S. presidential biography by Parson Weems (*The Life of Washington*, 1800) put the legend of George Washington and the cherry tree in our thinking. That tale became a part of elementary school history lessons. More seriously, in the nineteenth century, scientists would have taught that the "Caucasian" race was "more intelligent" than other "races," provable by scientific means. That also became part of the curriculum. Nobel Prize-winning geneticist James Watson raised a controversy in late 2007 by asserting that that information was still true (Dean, 2007). A leading Harvard astronomer was writing books about the canals of a lost civilization of Mars in the late 19th century (thus inspiring science fiction by H. G. Wells at least, a wonderful unintended consequence).

There is much uncertainty in knowledge and, therefore, a teacher must be humble. One of the great essays on the uncertainty of information and the hubris of knowledge, Guy Davenport's "Pergolesi's Dog" contains an absurdly sad story of how confused communication, convoluted information, and an intolerance toward "ignorance" and "error" destroyed a creative partnership. The essay is, as the title alludes, a literary "shaggy dog" story that is also a treatise on the subject of **error**. Davenport lists any number of errors one can find in standard reference works, the most hilarious example being a picture of French author Jules Verne with the caption identifying him as a Yellow-Headed Titmouse (a small bird, with a name that is quite confusing all by itself). There are certainly many errors in this primer, some more egregious than the others depending on the skill, knowledge, and attitude of the reader. But, as a teacher, I make no pretense of certainty, I only seek knowledge and wisdom.

Error
In developmental terms, error is a necessary part of experiential learning.

Further, it is important to note that knowledge has consequences, not all of them intended. After all, the inventor of dynamite endowed the Nobel Peace Prize. And genetic research carried out in the U.S. inspired and helped legitimate the Nazi Party's racial purity policies. Some of those Nazi scientists, such as Wernher Von Braun, returned the favor by developing the U.S. space program after World War II (Neufeld, 2007). The "intelligent design" promoters in the creationism versus evolution curriculum fight have co-opted liberal humanist Gerald Graff's pedagogical argument to "teach the differences" (1981). Intelligent design supporters have subverted Graff's "teach the differences" argument to push for the inclusion of creationism in the school science curriculum, so that students can be "taught the controversy." Evolutionary biologists and most other scientists say, "What controversy?" The issue of what question we take seriously is even more uncertain, depending on one's interests and one's intellectual stance.

Given the amount of uncertainty in everyone's lives, it would be better if everyone understood that error, not perfection, is humanity's true path. We spend most of our lives making wrong turns, not reading instructions, or misunderstanding what we hear. But that is how we learn. We learn by making mistakes. Learning something from experience includes learning from our mistakes. These are "errors of learning" that need to be distinguished from simple errors. When young children learn to speak, they make correct use of irregular verbs. They say "ate" for the past tense of "eat." When they learn about the rule for creating verbs in the past tense using "ed" in the early elementary grades, they frequently say they "eated" their meal. Then, through experience, they begin to understand both the general rule and the exceptions to the general rule and eventually go back to saying "ate" in regular discourse.

There are any number of cases, at any stage of development, as students learn generalizations or concepts, where they will get it "wrong." But they cannot get it right without getting it wrong first. And errors are more important in some contexts than others: spelling errors are much less important in the early drafts of writing when one is trying to get ideas down on paper than when one is preparing the document for publication. Developmentally, *everything* one learns about politics in third grade is "wrong" if one measures by the standards of an adult political operative.

While so much of what humans know is situated in a context, or contingent upon further study, or simply mistaken, it is clear that there are categories of knowledge that one must continue to refine if one is a professional in any field. We cannot wait for everything to be understood in any social practice but need to make do with what we know and strive for what we expect things to be. In the professional lives of teachers, this requires not only information and practice, but also a *stance*. Stance is a psychological concept that suggests both a manner of thinking and an attitudinal disposition. Teaching professionals need to adopt a stance that is experimental and scientific and at the same time traditionalist and humanistic. The latter comes from pursuing one's disciplinary understanding in a liberal arts and sciences context. The former comes from pursuing teacher research simultaneously with one's teaching.

Professionalization and the Teacher Researcher

Liminal
A state of existing in between two states of being, mentally characterized as ambiguous or indeterminate.

There is a notion of academic freedom in this country seemingly equal to protection of First Amendment rights. Certainly, teachers have been fired during periods of oppression, like the 1950s McCarthy era, but teaching tends to be protected. As a result, school can be what some ethnographers call a **liminal** space. Liminal spaces are places of transformation, temporarily placed outside of the normal boundaries of a society (Turner). While academic freedom for teachers is based on a legal construct from democratic reasoning, liminality is the basis for the "what if?" proposition—especially the "what if it was the other way around?" pedagogical question. We frequently ask students to imagine things differently than they are now. They can imagine things *wrongly* as well.

In pedagogically powerful classrooms, students read a variety of conservative voices, liberal voices, and radical voices. Students should hear voices of teachers, scholars, and researchers; other students; fictional creatures; dead white males; media reporters; paid shills; and related others and employ whatever knowledge is appropriate to the task at hand. Students need to compare different versions of knowledge and generate other possibilities as well and not take for granted the conditions of an argument set before them. Students read more than one version of the story; they travel the well-worn path *and* the road less traveled, not just one or the other.

The progenitor of modern pedagogy, John Dewey wrote "My Pedagogic Creed" in 1897. Most people who read the "Pedagogic Creed" would find little to argue with, though cultural and political conservatives frequently vilify Dewey, mostly in a **straw man argument**. By straw man argument, I mean attacking teaching practices that are loosely attributed to Dewey's influence rather than to anything Dewey actually wrote or did. Dewey, in work published during the first half of the 20th century, was savaging centuries of earlier school practice. Under the circumstances, it would be hard for anyone not to make some enemies among the authorities, many of whom are even today holding on to the humanistic traditions of the past. Indeed, many who attack Dewey's influence on modern school practices appear interested in returning to some mythical "good old days," though that argument is frequently ahistorical and the "good old days" and what made them "good" can be hard to pinpoint. Anyway, one should always beware of arguments citing past golden ages or guaranteeing future utopias.

Straw man argument
Setting up an imaginary adversary to make your argument stronger or to win the argument.

The point here is that John Dewey still speaks to us as democratic educators, certainly in the philosophical realm, in particular his observations about learning from the world as well as school. These are concerns of teaching that transcend disciplinary and even academic contexts. For example, one's cognitive schema is always dependent on ideas and experiences outside of the boundaries of the discipline. In some ways, one could argue that the development of expertise in a domain is a steady progression away from commonsense knowledge. But, even our beliefs and past experience shape our professional knowledge. As teachers we are always trying to live up to some ideal in our past, be it a real teacher or a fictional one. In teacher education, one never ceases to hear how a particular teacher inspired a student to pursue teaching.

Sometimes the teacher is a well-remembered caring individual, a teaching nun or a teacher from *Room 222* (the original school comedy-drama on television, not counting *Our Miss Brooks*). Or, sometimes, the role model is the drill instructor from *Full Metal Jacket* (Kubrik, 1987) or *An Officer and a Gentleman* (Hackford, 1982). These DIs, or drill *instructors*, are teachers in an educational institution. It is said that enlistments in the military always increase after the success of popular movies glamorizing service, such as *Top Gun* (Scott, 1987). *Top Gun* is another movie about school, in this case fighter pilot school, so there must be an educational intention to these films. That educative phenomenon is also true of other job movies, including teaching. There certainly tend to be more Hollywood movies about teaching when teaching is on the national agenda.

But, more importantly, there are basic cognitive schema, habits of mind, and essential cultural concepts that transcend disciplinary understanding. For example, most people learn new concepts through analogies with their prior knowledge or experience. The quality of the analogy is less important than that it is useful or effective on its own terms. "A child is like a flower" is not very scientific, but it provides a wonderful organic growth metaphor for learning and teaching. "Teaching is coaching" works for those who see coaching as one-on-one tutoring as well as for those who see themselves analogous to a marine drill sergeant-style football coach.

There has been much talk in recent decades about "teacher empowerment," a vision of raising teacher status and professionalism. The argument also assumes that teachers lack that status. There seem to be two branches of the empowerment model: in the first one teachers look more like university professors and in the second teachers gain self-efficacy through professional **guild** status. One will recognize the various ideological positions

Guild/Union

Originally, guilds were communities of practice that controlled economic conditions; modern labor unions negotiate economic and working conditions with management.

already outlined in these positions. Teacher empowerment is both an ideological and an epistemological argument.

In the first, the university-driven model, one hears strong support for "reflective" teaching and demands that the teacher serve as a "teacher-researcher" in her classroom. This version of empowerment envisions the improvement of the teacher's status, and of teaching in general, through the teacher assuming a role more like a university professor. The fact that a new teacher possesses a bachelor's degree and teaches the entire day, daily, is rarely contrasted with a new professor's recently earned Ph.D. and a teaching schedule that leaves time for research and writing. And so, somehow teachers must manage to act more like university professors and other professional researchers within their busy schedules and competing roles and functions. I suppose this is equivalent to the Jeffersonian ideal of the farmer-scholar and is more than most of us can attain.

But the classroom teacher must be reflective to grow. Given the core responsibilities of classroom teachers and the time constraints they work under, more realistic calls for the reflective teacher have focused on two strategies: (1) teachers writing about their experience as a means to reflection and (2) teachers engaging in practices that promote an informal sort of research, primarily focused on classroom activity and evaluation (Myers, 1985). The second is the more revolutionary, in that it requires teachers to think actively about the nature of learning experiences in their classrooms and to use sophisticated means of evaluation to account for student learning. By sophisticated, I mean a sophisticated understanding of evaluation, not a sophisticated knowledge of testing and statistics.

Teacher narrative
Teacher research built out of teacher stories, or research that uses teachers' accounts of practice.

Teacher inquiry
A teacher empowerment movement that asks teachers to design research, collect data, and interpret results without direction by outside researchers.

The first, focusing on teacher experience and development, is the one that has been more successful, at least as evidenced in the growing published accounts of teachers' lives. But there is a strong question about the pedagogical value of these narratives, since they normally are simply accounts of experience. **Teacher narrative** tends to focus on the teacher, and institutional concerns, whereas teacher research and **teacher inquiry** are student-centered. The two classic, paradigm-establishing teacher narratives from the 1960s, Jonathan Kozol's *Death at an Early Age* and Bel Kaufman's *Up the Down Staircase*, have nothing pedagogical about them, anymore than *The Blackboard Jungle* (Hunter, 1954).

However, teacher narrative is a powerful and significant function of the discourse of teaching. Teacher narrative influences teachers, parents, and policymakers. And, some teacher narratives are also actually teacher research, something that will be discussed in Chapter Six of this primer. This primer itself is a type of teacher narrative. For the time being, the key idea is that professionalization is based on teacher researcher insights, not just the folklore of teaching. Any book about teaching can be simply folklore, but no professional knowledge can be simply folklore.

A variation on this approach to teacher empowerment is supported by teacher unions and could be characterized as a guild model (referencing the medieval organizations of skilled craftsmen who regulated their professions). In this model, the craft knowledge, the teacher lore, becomes the currency of professionalism. Calls for more "realistic" teacher preparation frequently fall into this camp, as well as attempts to promote the economic interests of the teacher's union through paying union members to perform teacher development rather than contract workers, expanding their purview to include colleges. Unfortunately, some of the new school policies are promoting craft knowledge without any allegiance to the guild model. The new scripted lesson plans are an excellent example of "craft" knowledge being used to direct and control teachers rather than empower them.

In many cities, mayoral control removes the universities from the teacher development process while attacking the teacher unions as "obstructionist." Local authorities attempt to define the role of the teacher to meet the perceived needs of the school administration. That situation represents an attempt to control teaching behavior to direct the curriculum toward mass testing and curricular hegemony. These days, the "superintendent" or "chancellor" (frequently equated with, or actually designated, a CEO in a triumph of corporate thinking) is rarely even a school professional, let alone a teacher of long standing. The loss of experienced professionals in these positions has undermined teacher knowledge status at all levels of school administration.

The most important question for teachers concerning pedagogical options and imperatives in these cases is the question of authority. Are teachers there merely to enact the findings of professional researchers or, more precariously, the latest fads and trends in school management and political anxiety? Much of educational research proceeds from agendas and formulations that do not respond to teacher interests. Much of school administration looks at parental and taxpayer concerns to make policy.

For teachers to provide a knowledge base and a context for research seems to require a social and cultural sea change in the funding of research. The attempts to limit variables in behavioral research sometimes leave us with findings about stuff that appears insignificant for actual teaching. Pigeons pressing buttons to receive food or the social behavior of ants seem somewhat removed from sorting out the traumas of seventh-grade mathematics. And, some of that behavioral research appears to have no bearing on actual classrooms; research that focuses on one-on-one tutoring in an age of large class sizes seems a bit beside the point for the regular classroom. However, while classroom experience is necessary to good teaching, it is not sufficient to claim full authority over pedagogical inquiry. And, realistically, professional research can draw its assumptions only from the experience and knowledge of teachers who can communicate that knowledge. That articulation of knowledge begins with reflective practice.

Reflective practice is a teacher empowerment model of pedagogy, borrowed from multiple-profession studies of professional conduct (Schön, 1983). A reflective practice stance makes the teacher the final arbiter of the curriculum. Rather than teaching a prescribed curriculum, the teacher designs the curriculum, taking into account a number of variables. In reflective teaching classrooms, teachers take responsibility for assessing and evaluating both student performance and their own performance, for experimenting with various approaches to teaching, and for engaging in a professional dialogue with colleagues at a local, regional, and (inter)national level.

Reflective practice is a prerequisite to teacher research. Teacher research goes one step beyond reflective practice in that it assumes not only that the teacher makes curriculum through professional pedagogical thinking and action, but also that the teacher generates new knowledge about teaching in her own classroom. The teacher also connects with the larger community of research outside of her professional colleagues and assumes a responsibility for communicating or at least interacting with knowledge outside of the direct concerns of teaching a subject on a daily basis. However, teacher research stands in opposition to the tradition of researchers studying children and then telling teachers to incorporate the findings into their classrooms, or of other university and school staff developers working to improve teacher practice to be emulated by classroom teachers. Teacher researchers control themselves and the movement of the teaching profession and reverse the status of researcher in relation to the teacher (Kincheloe, 2006; Myers, 1985).

"Teacher researcher" is a status category that contains both cultural/social and academic/intellectual stances for defining teacher knowledge. Teacher research has been increasingly connected to the field of critical pedagogy, best realized in Joe Kincheloe's *Teachers as Researchers: Qualitative Inquiry as the Path to Teacher Empowerment* (2002). Kincheloe, a leading voice in critical pedagogy scholarship, claims, "Teacher researchers can revolutionize professional practice by viewing themselves as potentially the most sophisticated research instrument available" (2002, 52). Being a sophisticated research instrument is not an easy path given the social status of teachers in communities, but it is the only path to change for the profession. Even critical pedagogy, with its liberatory stance, cannot make teachers smarter or more sophisticated if they do not take a professional stance.

While reflective practice and teacher research are empowering to teachers, the role of critical pedagogy is to empower the students, teachers, and the institution of schooling. Critical pedagogy takes nothing for granted as to the content of the curriculum. Critical pedagogy is as skeptical about the liberal progressive end of the pedagogical curriculum as it is of the conservative (Freire, 1970). Critical pedagogues seek to unmask the tacit assumptions of schools in society as a means for empowering students in their school years and in their adult lives. Critical pedagogy calls to question the very assumption of authority by the teacher, seeking instead to pursue questions of equity and justice for all. And, of course, therein lies the conundrum regarding professionalism in the critical pedagogy paradigm. Joe Kincheloe's volume in the Peter Lang Primer series is a thoughtful and comprehensive look at the range of critical pedagogy, a field predicated on a critique and a prerequisite assumption of pedagogical knowledge (2008).

In the realm of pedagogy, critical pedagogy raises several epistemological questions beyond the political and cultural stance it takes. Critical pedagogy is part of the postmodern critique of modernism, but there remains a serious debate over the nature of **postmodernism** itself. Most postmodernists will argue that postmodernism has supplanted modernism, and that postmodernism is a new worldview. Others, some of them modernists, argue that postmodernism is a correction built into modernism. In other words, postmodernism is a self-correcting feedback loop contained within modernism. A third group, mostly traditionalists with modernist tendencies, see postmodernism as a reactionary movement fueled by foreign political ideologies and an overindulgence in academic argument at the expense of practical activity. One's attachment to critical pedagogy usually parallels one of the above orientations.

Postmodernism
Reactionary movement against modernism's basic tenets of breaking with the past, searching for new forms of expression, and embracing a scientific materialist unitary worldview.

It is difficult to escape critical pedagogy in any sensible discussion of schooling in our time. In fact, one can locate any number of critical pedagogy stances in this primer. But this primer assumes that critical pedagogy does not exist without the prior assertion of pedagogical principles and that critical pedagogy still requires understanding of past pedagogy and alternative pedagogies. After all, postmodernist stances are critiques of existing culture. In teaching, to be useful critical pedagogy, the critique must be part of teacher research and reflective teaching. Critical pedagogy without teacher research and pedagogical praxis is not pedagogy but merely policy or philosophy or even diatribe.

Mandated Curriculum and Standardized Testing

Mandated curriculum, and its handmaiden standardized testing, is where the other question about teacher knowledge and control of the curriculum enters. All teachers are subject to various mandated curricula and are held responsible for the teacher-directed curricula. Recent attempts to script teacher behavior and older attempts at individualized self-directed learning aside, no classroom teaching can occur without the agency of the teacher. The teacher can be revolutionary in many different ways in a classroom setting, but teachers can also hold the various elements of culture together. But, we teach in a context not wholly determined by us. Realistically, school teachers are hired into schools and students are required by law to attend: a teacher is not in her current situation because all the kids heard about how cool she was and just showed up to learn from her.

Mandated curriculum
Curriculum required by external authorities.

One of the central elements restricting teaching in the current cultural climate is the emphasis on evaluation. Evaluation is a very complex topic that has been seemingly reduced to basic information-based testing, using instruments produced by psychometric experts in testing companies. "Evaluation" in this model is used interchangeably with "accountability." This differs from the old emphasis on assessment to improve learning, the effective instruction tactic of providing frequent feedback on performance and understanding. Teachers use this formative assessment to better guide the students' learning experiences. Assessment as evaluation and/or accountability is a judgment about one's status and contains within it a notion of defined "success" and "failure." That is very different from a developmental, sustained growth metaphor.

Logically, one can see that core curriculum and mass testing assume that everyone will meet the same standard. Anyone familiar with psychometrics will tell you that such a system is workable (i.e., reliable) only if you set minimal standards. Unfortunately, since tests tend to influence the curriculum, the curriculum has become limited—reduced in content and expectation. A meaningless argument about covering the basics is used to support the new system, but the assumptions regarding "basics" and "building blocks" and "run before you can walk" and "prior knowledge" are based on adult models of learning. Developmentally, children learn holistically and frequently run as they learn to walk. During the process of literacy development, children do not write paragraphs, they write stories. Some children play beautiful music without reading the notes. Children steal your heart, or break your heart, long before they can reflect on their behavior. They play the video game long before they read the manual.

Most professionals believe their job is to teach, and not merely to judge. I personally believe that especially mindless "evaluation" statements such as "these kids can't write" should be grounds for dismissal. To argue that kids do not know anything defies the simplest of logics. And yet, it is not unusual to hear teachers make comments such as "these kids are not prepared to learn what I have to teach them, so I just gave up hoping they'll learn anything." I suppose that statement is the equivalent of a physician saying that all patients are going to die, so why treat them anyway? Or, better, a physician explains the death of a patient by saying the person was sick before she treated him.

It is interesting that the popular argument for prior knowledge, as articulated by E. D. Hirsch in *Cultural Literacy*, drew its rationale from research on schema theory but was turned into an over-determining explanation for "failure." Arguing that prior knowledge research proved that what we know affects what we can learn, Hirsch simplified the notion to a list of information that all Americans needed to know to be able to learn anything. The problem was that while cognitive science research on prior knowledge argued in terms of what they called mental schema (one needed to know, for example, what a horse was to understand riding, or certain ethical assumptions to understand the "moral" of a story), Hirsch turned this complex mental and behavioral activity into storing information on a hard drive in a computer (as he characterized the nature and functioning of the human brain in his book).

Prior knowledge is an important part of teaching method, but cultural literacy itself is a very small and possibly misleading representation of prior knowledge for teaching purposes. The point here is that the "content" standards movement derives essentially from the same impulse as the cultural literacy movement, and that sort of simplistic reasoning (kids "fail" because they *lack* information, the so-called deficit model) drives some important curricular and pedagogical thinking. The cultural literacy branch of the content standards movement also tends to promote an anachronistic return to pre-multicultural times, since it is based on a supposedly historical argument of perennial American cultural themes.

But knowledge is not permanently "stored" in the brain. It is organized and understood as memory only within mental schema. As one experiences more and learns more concepts and facts, the prevailing mental schema used to organize and recall your knowledge changes, which, in effect, changes how you understand other memories of experience and knowledge. Knowledge is fluid. But, more importantly, knowledge is "situational." The real lesson for pedagogy behind the schema theory research is that prior knowledge determines the meaning one derives from the new knowledge. Learning is not as simple as one "gets it" or not. Pedagogically, prior knowledge that the student already possesses could interfere with learning a new concept or tacitly assimilating new information. Moreover, some prior knowledge is useful only for the immediate situation at hand, for which the teacher or circumstance provides the prior knowledge.

In planning a classroom experience, schema theory tells us that activating the student's prior knowledge engages the student in learning the new knowledge. Asking students for an example from their own experience that parallels the information or skills to be taught is a standard practice. "Have your ever felt like you had no friends and that nobody cared about you?" one could ask before reading a story about a lonely person. That also activates the emotive elements in the experience. In science, one can ask students for their commonsense understandings of natural phenomena before teaching the scientific explanations. In most cases, since so much of folklore actually interferes with learning scientific concepts, the teacher can directly address schema elements (prior knowledge) that might undermine scientific knowledge (Cobern, 2000).

The essential argument for cultural literacy, like the "cultural heritage" model before it, is a political argument for a common culture, and not a serious cognitive theory about prior knowledge's role in developing mental schema. It is a common culture that can be used to test the population in standardized ways, and in ways that can have "benchmarks" and "standards" and "consequences" for those who do not meet those standards. The more obvious political and cultural objection to the cultural literacy curriculum is that one curriculum serves all, and that no single cultural model can serve, or tame, a multicultural world. On a practical level, much of the cultural literacy material is formalistic knowledge in any case: the multiplication and division of fractions is the best example. I personally have yet to find a simple functional use for that knowledge: the only "practical" examples usually involve fractional gallons of milk, which would figure better if converted to ounces, and kilograms (from a study of *Chinese* teachers) of sugar, certainly better when converted to grams for simple division.

Yet, division and multiplication of fractions has become a standard item on teacher tests. Addition of fractions was used to ambush the head of the NYC teachers' union in a public debate over testing on a radio show: "What is 1/3 and 1/4?," asked the radio host, as the teachers' union head sputtered in embarrassment (Herszenhorn, 2006). A better question to school officials might be "Why is multiplication of fractions considered core knowledge when knowledge of electrical wiring is not?" Is not the second one a more useful set of understandings, even without the practical skills, in our current information-based, mediated world than formal mathematical knowledge? Those questions would show that the moderator was interested in the larger educational questions rather than in attempting to embarrass and belittle the head of the teachers' union. And, that question of the purpose of knowledge is precisely the question that needs to be asked on a regular basis.

As for evaluation becoming a strong determiner of curriculum, the biggest topic recently in P-16 education is "evidenced-based instruction" tied to questions about educational evaluation and assessment, especially high-stakes testing. The assertion appears to be that the formative and informal assessment that teachers engage in is not very "scientific," and teachers are not basing their curricular and pedagogical judgments on "evidence" of student learning. The "evidence" standard in this situation moves from the teacher's judgment to the evidence on standardized tests. In this world of increasing litigation, one cannot help but wonder if the use of the word "evidence" is merely a coincidence. Certainly, if one were to use student test scores to fire teachers, it carries more weight if it is based on "evidence."

Much of the evidence-based push is an attempt to undermine teacher authority. Teachers tend to think of assignments as teaching tools more than as evaluation tools, while policymakers appear to believe that all school activity is ipso facto evaluative. Teachers engage in both formative and summative evaluation, but policymakers appear to see all evaluation as summative, preferably high-stakes where a test score can be used to make important decisions about a student's future. Teachers see themselves as making assignments and designing activities, policymakers apparently view all this activity as "collecting evidence." It goes without saying, the focus on evaluation puts the cart before the horse, but that is inevitable in the Tyler-rationalized world of technical-rational reasoning.

Certainly, teaching proceeds better if focused on instructional planning first and evaluation second, thereby putting the horse back in its rightful place. Also, putting pedagogy first requires the teacher to address teaching rather than prejudging students on their lack of prior knowledge and experience and declaring them either hopeless or lazy. Planning for teaching takes seriously the students' prior learning and experiences, while defining one's own professional responsibilities. Evaluation is clearly built into effective lessons because the students have responsibility for producing knowledge, and teachers have responsibilities to teach and provide feedback.

As mentioned above, some of the curriculum is required by legislative mandate or local requirements of some sort. These days much is made of the *legal* requirements surrounding the new curricula in many states. Conservative state legislators are frequently heard threatening teachers and professors with "consequences" if they do not teach the new state-mandated curriculum. This cultural thrust is what I have come to call the criminalization of teaching. Yet, even in this climate, there is no requirement for understanding legal issues in teaching and schooling for teacher certification, except as it relates to special education or special populations (PL 94–142, etc.). Professional pedagogical knowledge requires an understanding of all the legal issues related to teacher and student rights and the conduct of inquiry, especially as it relates to human subjects research.

Too much can be made of the "legal" responsibilities of teachers to the mandated curriculum. Most of the actual legal requirements of teaching are associated with criminal activity that must be reported in any case, such as child abuse or drug dealing and/or consumption. Teachers being prosecuted for not teaching phonics or "traditional" American history or evolution appears unlikely, though the Scopes "monkey" trial is not that far in the past. And, remember, Scopes and evolutionary theory did not win in that case.

Despite all of this, most of what teachers are worried about ("fear" seems a bit much) is the mandated curriculum. What teachers are most likely to care about personally and professionally is the teacher-selected curriculum, the "creative" part of our work in the classroom. However, the multilayered mandated curriculum—curriculum required of the teacher and school from outside authorities—is a responsibility to which the teacher must attend. Most states now require some sort of curriculum framework, called content standards or standards framework, for each of the grade levels and the various disciplines. There are third grade language arts standards and high school English standards and so on throughout for the various subjects in the K-12 system.

Rather than pursue a national curriculum, as is the case in most Western democracies, the United States stuck to the federalism (states' rights) pattern and made the standardization of the curriculum a state responsibility. What was lost in the debate was that the shift to state-level responsibility was a fundamental shift away from the control of schools by local community boards. In the 1990s, even most of the responsibility for funding schools was shifted from local to state jurisdiction (the resultant reduction and redistribution of school funding are part of that trend). The shift from local to state was probably even more important than the Elementary and Secondary Education Act (ESEA) of the 1960s, which marked the first big influx of federal funding into (and, therefore, control over) K-12 schools.

Federal contracts were awarded during the 1980s for the development of "model" state curriculum frameworks. Most of those frameworks did become models for individual states for setting standards for teaching, curriculum, and student performance during the 1990s. After 2000, the ESEA became the No Child Left Behind legislation mandating major testing initiatives and severe penalties for students, teachers, and schools (e.g., schools were required to be dissolved for poor performance if the overall school performance on the standardized tests was not at acceptable levels). While this "teach 'em and test 'em" model appears fairly straightforward, there are several as yet unresolved issues at the heart of the standards and testing movement that affect the teacher and pedagogical thinking.

Content standards
Testing focused on individual knowledge.

Performance standards
Multiple measure assessment, including group assessment, employing exhibitions of knowledge and skills.

The first problem is the distinction between **performance standards** and **content standards** in curriculum and testing. The great revolution of the 20th century was the development of performance standards. During the 19th century, curriculum was based primarily on the content of the curriculum. The first movement toward standardizing the college preparatory curriculum for the growing country was in the drafting of the Uniform Lists that provided guidance from the eastern colleges, primarily at the request of the geographically and culturally distant western schools, regarding the titles students should read to prepare for college. The nineteenth-century tests measured knowledge of specific books (though the list could change yearly) and specific content knowledge such as author's biographies, formal definitions of grammar and parts of speech, or mathematical formulae and specific knowledge about scientific topics.

With the development of intelligence testing (IQ, or intelligence quotient, the relationship of one's "mental" age to one's chronological age) in the early part of the 20th century, the psychometric movement reinvented tests to be more "fair" by focusing on specific intellectual skills (this is where we get "critical thinking," e.g.) rather than specific content. It was believed that the performance-testing base of the new tests (such as the SAT, which came to dominate after the 1930s) was more democratic in that it tested everyone on the basis of their "mental abilities" rather than their knowledge (which could be culturally biased or class-based) and assumed that these general mental abilities also transcended specific content (the theory of "transferability" of general mental skills). The movement from content to performance represents an epistemological difference in what constituted knowledge.

Performance testing dominated teaching in the United States until very recently. With the exception of a few old-fashioned content tests, such as the New York State Regents Examinations, most testing in this country was accomplished through performance-based tests such as the Iowa Test of Basic *Skills* or the Scholastic *Aptitude* Test (as the SAT used to be entitled). The key words in the titles of the tests described mental and behavioral processes rather than knowledge of specific content. As a result, teachers learned to teach "critical thinking" skills, comprehension skills in reading, grammar and usage in context, mathematical and inductive reasoning, and word recognition skills (context and sound as well as structural characteristics such as prefixes and suffixes and Latin and Greek roots—rather than memorizing lists of words). Much of what passes for pedagogy today is a result of the influence of these performance tests.

Two sorts of criticisms have led to the reduction of influence of these types of tests, one internal and the other a reactionary movement to reassert content testing as the standard. The internal criticism became paramount after composition became a staple of the curriculum mandates during the 1980s. The argument was simple and elegant: the SAT test of writing ability contained no requirement to write anything. To repeat, the performance test of writing did not ask the student to perform any writing. Instead, the test of writing ability mainly tested grammar and "standard" usage knowledge in a multiple-choice format. This made sense to test makers, since mass standardized testing was legitimated on the reliability of the multiple-choice format.

But the reliability of the format caused problems for the validity of the task. It was not an authentic test of writing ability. However, as long as it was demonstrated that grammar and usage knowledge correlated with college grades in freshman English, the SAT multiple-choice test was sufficient. The nature of writing instruction changed following British research in the 1960s and 1970s combined with an emphasis on post-industrial information society curriculum imperatives in the U.S. (Barnes et al., 1971; Britton, 1970; 1976; Britton et al., 1975; Dixon, 1968;). When the teaching of writing shifted from an emphasis on formal correctness to a focus on invention and revising, the nature of the assessment had to change to reflect "authentic" writing (Berlin, 1987). On the other hand, only recently has the essay (and other writing forms) become standard for college admission testing as it was back in the 19th century—though it had unofficially continued throughout the century masquerading as the personal essay in college applications.

The second part of the shift in recent years is the move from mass testing, standardizing testing to inform about the behavior and ability of large numbers of students, to an emphasis on individual performance. While the SAT (and the ACT for that matter) has always marked individual scores, each is usually "norm-referenced," meaning you are measured against those who took the test when you did. The individual is measured against the peer group. The origin of mass testing, situated in a performance paradigm, was to group individuals within peer group norms. The test did not measure the individual against anyone but his/her peers and, therefore, was a relative measure. In classrooms, this produced the well-known notion of "grading on the curve," with reference to the bell-shaped curve that was the ideal of normative testing.

The other main category of testing is called criterion-referenced, in which the individual test taker must meet a specific established standard of performance. Most of the new state assessments are criterion-referenced tests, tied to the standards in the new state curriculum frameworks. New York State was able to use the Regents for this purpose, since the trend is back to the content standards that produced this state test in the first place. Other states either adopted older tests or developed a brand-new criterion-referenced set of tests to demonstrate the success of their new content standards within a standardized curriculum to respond to federal mandates (but only if they required federal financing assistance). The SAT and ACT continue as college admissions examinations, but now students must also take the state tests to graduate from high school. The first two are entrance examinations for those who wish to pursue postsecondary education; the state test is a high-stakes exit examination that threatens to withhold the high school diploma from students who do not "measure up."

One other older test remains, one that developed out of President Nixon's 1969 demand for an assessment tool to validate federal funding of the ESEA. The National Assessment of Educational Progress (NAEP) is a descriptive test that provides a "snapshot" of student *performance* at several crucial points in their schooling. The NAEP does not test everyone, nor are individual test scores reported. A representative sample of students (representatives of various demographic traits who are chosen randomly from within their categories) takes the test every several years to see how American students are doing *on average* in several key academic and intellectual areas. The NAEP pioneered several performance assessment techniques, in particular in writing assessment, with attempts to focus on authentic and valid performance in various subjects.

The NAEP still carries influence. When one reads about the national performance of eighth-grade students in mathematics, for example, it is usually in the latest report of the NAEP results. The NAEP is important in that it provides a sense of how the nation is doing overall and provides some comparative data for policymakers. If the eighth-grade mathematics scores remain stagnant for a decade, or if certain racial or ethnic groups are performing poorly as a group, then that usually results in some sort of policy mandate to improve instruction in that area or for that afflicted group.

All of this evaluation and study sometimes results in what Judith Summerfield calls "barking statistics" (personal communication). Dialogue stops when someone shouts out a statistic that is supposed to change the focus of the discussion, or to delegitimize the topic at hand. Someone else will bark out another statistic in response to the first. Barking statistics are everywhere these days, from Fox News and CNN to senators and congressman on C-SPAN, to medical doctors on morning television, to the front page of most print media. But, when these statistics are not used simply to bully, they represent efforts to construct knowledge.

The nature of knowledge, group or individual, personal or formal, experiential or vicarious, is not something a teacher can take for granted. Teachers are knowledge workers, knowledge is what we make as well as transmit. Evaluation models are frequently promoted that attempt to wrest this authority away from teachers, but in the end the classroom is a world of ideas, or not, because the teacher has made it possible for those ideas to thrive and grow. Students learn content and skill from teachers, but in the end it is the engaging of the metacognitive, learning to think about thinking, that is the best education teachers provide. Metacognition is not available through a curriculum governed by standardized testing (except for test-taking skills). The educational result of limiting students to standardized curriculum and high-stakes tests is cynicism among students about the value of knowledge. Teaching is about taking knowledge and knowing seriously.

Glossary

Error—A word so important to human experience and meaning that it has different meanings in many different domains. In developmental terms, error is a necessary part of experiential learning. In formal knowledge terms, errors are conflated with mistakes. Error is also used in experimental science to distinguish between a true value and a measured value, further contextualized as either random or systemic (predictable) errors.

Guild/Union—Originally, guilds were communities of practice that controlled economic conditions surrounding craft and professional activities. Modern labor unions negotiate economic and working conditions with management.

Liminal—A state of existing in between two states of being, mentally characterized as ambiguous or indeterminate.

Mandated curriculum—Curriculum required by external authorities that teachers must account for in their classroom teaching and integrate into their classroom curriculum.

Performance standards/content standards—Standards are statements of student achievement expectations and establish specific thresholds of knowledge and performance. The split between content standards and performance standards is an ideological split. Content standards promote testing focused on individual exhibitions of knowledge. Performance standards advocates argue for a wider range of assessment, including group assessment, as exhibitions of student knowledge and skill; they would, for example, prefer a portfolio assessment over a standardized test of knowledge. Performance standards tend to resemble older style assessments in their preference for mental habits and functions assessments rather than the testing of specific mandated knowledge.

Postmodernism—A reactionary movement against modernism's basic tenets of breaking with the past, searching for new forms of expression, and embracing a scientific materialist unitary worldview. Postmodernism manifests itself by mixing genres and styles, mining and "quoting" the past, and arguing for multiple worldviews.

Stance—A psychological term suggesting a predisposition or a point of reference that is intentional and rationalized.

Straw man argument—Setting up an imaginary adversary to make your argument stronger or to win the argument. John Dewey, a strong and sophisticated intellectual, is usually represented through the most meager of progressive education examples or through fictional attributes of certain kinds of progressive schooling, when opponents are attempting to refute Dewey's philosophy.

Teacher inquiry—A teacher empowerment movement that asks teachers to design research, collect data, and interpret results without direction by outside researchers. Called "action research" or "teacher research" in other contexts, teacher inquiry assumes that classroom-specific or realistic research can come only from teachers themselves.

Teacher narrative—Teacher research built out of teacher stories, or research that uses teachers' accounts of practice. Also includes teacher autobiography and teacher lore and can serve as a medium for reflective practice.

CHAPTER SIX

The Language of Pedagogy: Texts, Narratives, and Discourses

Language is the constitutive human activity; it is what defines us as a species. Most evolutionary biologists and archaeologists tie the development of language in humans to the "great leap forward" of the Upper Paleolithic period (50,000–70,000 years ago) that also marks a transformative growth in the diversity and efficiency of tool making, and, just as important, the first appearance of art (Spencer Wells, 2002, p. 85). It seems to me there is much to be gleaned from that version of the human story. In any case, language is central to modern human understanding and functioning and, necessarily, should be a central concern of formal teaching.

Orality
The study of the rules and contexts of spoken language.

Talk—that is, **orality**—is a big part of our lives; talk accounts for an overwhelming majority of verbal communication (Ong, 1982). Talk is not the only means of communication, nor the only means of representing understanding, but it has always had a big role in teaching and learning. Up until the 1920s, most teachers taught through the "recitation" method. Students were asked to stand and formally recite various forms of knowledge in the classroom. As for earlier evaluation methods, not until the 1860s did most examinations in colleges even

Literacy
The ability to read and write. The definition of literacy changes with the times, and throughout history most of humankind has been illiterate.

Linguistic/ Psycholinguistic
The study of language is linguistics; the study of language learning and use, and its relationship to thinking, is psycholinguistics.

Textuality
A postmodern theory situating the object of study as a "text" that is always unfinished and without the possibility of full comprehension.

begin to become written examinations; almost all examinations were oral. Modern written examinations started with the first national efforts at college entrance examinations beginning in the 1870s, though much of classroom evaluation continued to revolve around oral language. But a major change came to instruction in schools from the scientific management and the social efficiency movement that were part of the Progressive Era. Text, and its attendant **literacy**, became essential for the new scientific, industrial, efficiency-oriented, progressive world. The grand move to focus on scientific studies of reading, especially more efficient, faster *silent* reading, originates in this Progressive Era.

In the classroom, much of learning and teaching still takes place through the medium of language, though language is much more than a simple medium in understanding concepts or in managing our environments. Even mathematics and art teachers, proponents of the quantitative and the visual, do most of their teaching practice through **linguistic** means. The use of oral language among most disciplines is the same, though textual representation marks important differences. And, the value and possibility of textual use in one's teaching is tied to the theory of **textuality** you embrace. Simply taking text at face value is no way to run a classroom.

Mathematics requires special type fonts that look like hieroglyphics to most non-mathematicians; art books are full of visual information, that is, pictures. Social studies texts increasingly focus on "reproductions" of "authentic" "source" "documents" (all problematic terms), and that language requires scaffolded and structured reading experiences, including advanced organizers, glossaries, and textual study. Words have common meanings (one simply assumes that you and the speaker share a common meaning) and special meanings, especially in academic, technical, or professional discourse. In every instance, the first task of teaching is defining our terms and using language appropriate to the task and audience.

The biggest difference since the 1920s has been the increasingly sophisticated text material, normally embodied in "textbooks" or "teaching materials." It is interesting that, though the book has remained generally the same since early seventeenth century, various conventions have shifted. The 19th central novel was normally illustrated; in the 20th century, the novel loses its pictures. The trend is so pervasive that classic 19th-century novels are reprinted with only the text; generations of readers did not seem to know that Mark Twain's books contained hundreds of illustrations unless they had access to a 19th-century edition or a facsimile copy. Strangely, the modern editions of Charles Dickens' novels always retained some illustration. The separation of pictures from text begins after the invention of film, so that may be one of the reasons for the deliberate rejection of the other. Film itself was fundamentally transformed by the introduction of sound approximately thirty years after the appearance of the new nickelodeons, so much so, in fact, that 80 percent (roughly the survival rate of medieval manuscripts) of all silent films are lost to us.

Speaking of film, it must be noted that this is the age of "mass media" or "multimedia" or, as Marshall McLuhan originally styled the notion, the "global village" where "the medium is the message" (*Understanding Media: The Extensions of Man*, 1964). We now inhabit a complex culture that produced photography 175 years ago, film 100 years ago, and television 50 years ago. And yet, we still build most of schooling around textual literacy. It remains a traditional textual literacy as well, when textual literacy is now much more complex than in the pre–mass media era. But first one needs to explore the nature of language and then return to the new definitions of language and representation represented by the various new media. The technological utopian ideal is convergence—the integration of voice, data, video, and Internet in a single source wireless digital environment. But, in the end, language, especially text, remains central to teaching, regardless of the medium, even though the medium changes the message and even the nature of language itself.

Language also has a history, some of which is useful for teachers to know. It is interesting that our complaints about "rote" learning simply employ the Middle English word for "heart," as in "learning by heart." One wonders if this remnant form of the expression remains with us because it is old-fashioned and contains a negative connotation that learning something by heart undermines as a sentiment. "Learning something by heart" sounds very powerful and even intimate; learning by rote evokes drudgery and disconnectedness. Language constitutes a layered and evocative medium.

Sometimes the history of language can teach us something profound. Predictably, there is a "great debate" in this country between the notion of "prescriptive" language teaching and "descriptive" language teaching. The debate is sometimes evoked also as "grammar versus usage" or "formal versus functional" or "logical versus historical," just to demonstrate the slipperiness and ubiquity of this dualism. While the debate might appear academic on the surface, it is the basic ingredient for several violent disagreements over school practice that in recent years has focused on "whole language" instruction in elementary schools, and over any number of issues regarding other pedagogical practices.

When one studies the history of language, one sees that language changes over time: before the fifteenth century, most residents of England spoke one of several different dialects, each very different from the modern textual form of English. This is true of all the languages of Europe and most other places around the world. Since the 18th century, speakers of English in England and the United States have been trying to stop the language from changing and have been attempting to regularize the language. Hence, the development of grammar books, dictionaries, and spelling books. Written language grammar and formal usage rules set by formal or informal groups are always attempts, in early grammarians' terms, to "fix and ascertain" the language.

Standardization
Establishing agreed upon technical standards in any circumstance or situation.

Standardization does not need to be intentional or formal. One can better see the importance of the *publication* of Shakespeare's plays and the publication of King James translation of the Bible and the Book of Common Prayer in the early 17th century as standardizing influences on modern written English, since they became "classic" texts of a national culture that influenced everyone who could read. In this country, Noah Webster's dictionary attempted to define American English and, true to his puritan Yankee dislike of European affectation, he removed the "u" from English words such as "honour" to make the words more American, that is, more logical, simple, and commonsensical. Webster's spellers and readers were patriotic statements as well as literacy primers.

What is important here is that oral language continues to change, though, through the efforts of linguists and dictionary publishers and the schoolbook makers, the written language has stabilized to some degree. The situation in world English is now challenging that stability, though the written form of the language is further standardized by any number of influences including Internet search engines. One could legitimately argue that although the English language, the language with the largest lexicon among earthly languages, has been standardized, it continues to grow in vocabulary. No one is trying to make English *smaller*, though there were several attempts in the 20th century to make it simpler, most notably the Basic English movement, a very scientific attempt to regularize and simplify English grammar and syntax lead by English philosopher, pedagogue, and linguist I. A. Richards, out of which developed the highly influential field of semantics.

English is a difficult language to master, mainly because of its complicated roots. At root a Germanic language (Anglo-Saxon or Old English), English was layered over by Old French (a Romance language) in the years following the Norman Conquest of 1066 and was then further transformed by the addition of Latinate vocabulary beginning in the 12th-century ecclesiastical and proto-humanist mini-renaissance (see Cantor, 1994). Over time, the influences melded and the language changed, even passing through the Great Vowel Shift of the 15th century during which the whole system of English pronunciation changed. Out of that process, and the brilliant textual influences mentioned above, emerged what we now call modern English.

But, in some ways, the history of the language teaches us only what should be obvious: language is subject to change, especially oral language. But the *conventions* of textual language change as well: The semicolon is a recent invention. The preference for active versus passive voice, if not a modern scientific choice, is certainly a pragmatist notion. Older texts are full of digressions while modern text is very "stripped down" or straightforward. The nature of authorial voice has changed fundamentally over the centuries, though the authority of voice has remained constant in schoolbooks.

Even the value of language changes over time, for various reasons. The world is losing many of its smaller languages as colonialism has spread the major languages around the world even in the "postcolonial" world. The Internet is the most recent culprit is spreading English as the lingua franca (a reference to when French was the language of world diplomacy). But the best recent example of changing fortunes is the dethronement of German as the language of science; a scientist could hardly be called a scientist in the 19th century unless he read German. German was the most important foreign language among the educated classes in the United States before World War I. Anti-German sentiment emanating from World Wars I and II has virtually eliminated German from American schools. The shift of scientific leadership to the United States in the 20th century (ironically led by many former natives of Germany such as Einstein and Von Braun) has made English the new language of science. This situation leads to certain ironies in other symbol systems. American scientists use the metric system even though the U.S. does not formally employ it, being one of the very few countries that do not. Here is a case where the high status value of scientific representation is undermined by cultural conservatism.

As for language studies in the 20th century, Latin suffered a resounding defeat after many centuries of hegemony. The great universities of England did not even offer courses of study in English literature until World War I (Potter, 1937). When Matthew Arnold gave the first lecture on Modernism in Literature at Oxford in the 1860s, he orated in Latin. One spoke and read and wrote Latin and Greek in higher education until the 20th century, a carryover from the use of Latin as the international language of scholarship promoted by the Roman Catholic Church, though it was coincidentally the language of the Greek and Roman authors who wrote the classics of the Renaissance revival of secular learning. The Carnegie Foundation for the Advancement of Teaching's 1908 study of the "efficiency" of Latin study was the death knell for the subject in American secondary and postsecondary education (Pritchett). This was the first important case of modern science defeating a traditional school practice. Add this change to the previous development of the kindergarten, based on European child study by scientists such as Montessori, and one can see that "the times were a changin'" long before Bob Dylan sang about it in the 1960s.

However, all of the current language in the social discussion boils down to a distinction between a "prescriptive" approach to language (the way language should be spoken or written) and a "descriptive" approach (the way language is spoken and written). The debate flares up around new dictionaries and their inclusions of new words in each new edition; it ignites over the tendency to change a word's original part of speech (especially turning neologism nouns into verbs, as in "I googled him and found out he's blogging when he's not just hanging with his friends"). English teachers are always accused of being grammar police, but English majors who have any linguistic knowledge tend to be more liberal about language than most other people.

All that English teachers ever hear from other teachers is how bad the "grammar" in student papers is, as if the English teacher is the only one who can do anything about that. You assign the paper; you need to teach the skills or set the appropriate standards. Do not expect that to be done somewhere else, by somebody else, in some magical way. And do not blame the students because "they can't write." All language is situated, and the standards are determined by the context of language use. Nobody writes a formal letter to a friend, but that should be obvious. Many kids fail to turn in proper writing for school assignments because they do not know how to do what the teacher is asking. The simplest thing to do, of course, is teach the discourse of your academic field to your students. Art teachers do not teach students to write biology laboratory reports. The problem with most history papers, which always seem to require the largest number of pages of all school assignments, has little to do with the students' lack of grammar knowledge.

In the end, the "prescriptive versus descriptive" debate divides into *two* central parts: one of them is the debate over grammar versus usage, the other is over the nature of language learning in children and adolescents. It is important for all teachers to understand the conditions of this debate, rather than blindly take sides from an ideological perspective. In some ways, this debate is a repeat of the logical versus psychological organization of the curriculum debate first articulated by Dewey. But, mostly, it is an essential element in pedagogical content knowledge that should influence all of teaching practice.

In recent years, literacy has become a requirement of new teachers of all disciplines and backgrounds, simply and functionally because literacy appears to be a barrier to learning content. The discussion that follows is not meant to be useful only for English teachers or reading teachers in the elementary school, but for all teachers who hope to bring more literacy instruction to the students. Some illustrations from the English curriculum may help illuminate the unarticulated assumptions teachers of mathematics or physical education might need to better understand their own literacy training and literacy practices (Purves & Niles, 1984).

There also exists a seemingly simple curriculum discussion that masks major ideological differences simply in the naming practices. Understanding the relationship between the naming practices and the pedagogy at least keeps a teacher from working at cross-purposes to one's own intentions. However, there is a specific knowledge about language development that should be the domain not only of English teachers, since all teachers employ tacit linguistic theory in their classrooms in both actions and intentions. All teachers are, as the saying goes, teachers of literacy, even if they do not want to be. The examples that follow show the complexity in one domain, English, but students of any discipline will recognize the structure and fill in the blanks from mathematics or social studies or art or physical education.

On the simplest level, the distinction between process and content approaches in English can be seen in two key ways of representing the curriculum of English teaching. One is a representation as psychological and behavioral processes: reading, writing, speaking, and listening (and sometimes viewing). The reciprocal representation, the content approach, includes a range of topics: language, literature, and composition (and sometimes media). The former is a psychologically organized view while the latter is a logically organized view of the English curriculum.

The psychologically organized curriculum focuses on the learner and the socio-psycholinguistic processes in which the learner engages, while the logically organized curriculum focuses on the content to be learned. But the process versus content debate also implies a perceptual distinction between seeing children as failed adults, based on what Stephen Tchudi calls "anticipatory remediation," versus seeing children as growing through trial and error, doing work appropriate to their ages, employing the "developmental" approach. In one view, children are measured against an adult standard (guaranteeing that they will come up short, i.e., as deficient adults), in the other the children are measured against their peers (knowledge of what is "normal" to know for students of a certain age derived from educational research).

In other words, the psychologized approach to the language curriculum contains within it an attitude toward learning and students that is opposed to the attitude toward learning suggested by those relying solely on a logical organization of the curriculum. Those concerned solely with the logical organization of the English curriculum are concerned with the state of knowledge, the nature of content in the field, and the correctness of the language. Developmental teaching perspectives are more attuned to the learner understanding important content within the context of meaningful behavior.

Importantly, the dialectic between English conceived as *process* (reading, writing, speaking, listening, viewing, i.e., the psychological organization) and English conceived as *product* (language, literature, composition, media, i.e., the logical organization) provides the formula for change and development in the curriculum. To see language teaching simply as one or the other limits either the subject or the learner. The demands of one cannot take precedence over the other. This relationship illustrates the necessary reciprocal structure of the two worldviews, the two epistemologies, and the two approaches to teaching children.

But, the teacher needs to understand the psychological, the piece that is missing in most teacher preparation outside of English, and in alternate route preparation that does not focus on pedagogical content knowledge. One of the best examples of how the psychological transforms the curriculum is in elementary school language development and literacy. Prior to the language teaching revolution that occurred after the Anglo-American conference in 1966 that introduced American educators to the work of the University of London's Institute of Education directed by James Britton, the elementary language arts curriculum, simply called reading at the time, was organized very "logically" (Britton, 1970). The reading curriculum, defined by the basal reader, was developed around research in reading, but even that research, centered on word counts and simplified vocabulary and syntax, was logically rather than psychologically organized. Logically, students in elementary schools also focused on writing individual sentences "correctly" before learning to write single paragraphs and then five-paragraph essays. The problem with that approach is that the last thing anyone learns to write well is the sentence. Also, the emphasis on individual sentences and paragraphs is a bit wrongheaded: one sentence always implies another, and a paragraph always *requires* at least two, rhetorically and logically.

Rather than study how children actually read, researchers in the first half of the 20th century studied adult use of language and developed a school curriculum from those findings. For example, the Dolch Word List, a compilation of the 220 most frequently used words in English speech (including words such as *a* and *the*), became the basis for the development of controlled vocabulary readers. The assumption was that words most frequently used by adults constituted the foundation of all reading and language instruction. The "Dick and Jane" books (e.g., See Spot run) and, in a wonderful subversion of his publisher's requirement regarding limited vocabulary, the Dr. Suess books (Theodore Geisel) were both written out of the limited vocabulary.

The British educational researchers of the1950s and 1960s had taken another approach to studying child language: observe and record child language and generalize about learning from that data. They found that kids did not learn the 220 most-used words first, basal readers used unreal language that undermined literacy, language play was essential, and reading and writing could be taught better simultaneously instead of reading preceding writing. They developed a new descriptive vocabulary to reference the new field of psycholinguists (now socio-psycholinguistics) and hypothesized about the full range of language development and, in a nod to pragmatist thinking, language *use*. These were functional, not formal, theories of language developmental, theorized out of classrooms and children's behavior. They paved the way for holistic practice and the process method.

Out of that research came the whole language approach to elementary language arts, but that has split into method and philosophy. Whole language philosophy, rather than method, has been the Ground Zero of neoconservative attacks. This philosophical debate is sometimes correctly regarded as the "correctness versus errors of learning" argument. We need room in the curriculum to learn from our mistakes, say whole language advocates. Things are either right or wrong, says the correctness advocate; words can be spelled only one way. This argument, whether you are an English teacher or a mathematics teacher caught up in the quantitative reasoning debate, remains the same. The underlying assumptions about language (and mathematics) are central to our other personal and unarticulated learning theories.

This philosophical and epistemological debate, played out along political lines, can be complicating for our language pedagogy. The idea of a "correct" language carries over into policies regarding multiple languages and bilingualism. Though there are four major language groups in the Americas, and most educated citizens of other countries appear to be multilingual, the U.S. remains steadfast in its official commitment to teaching only English in schools, providing only limited transitional instruction. Most of bilingualism policy has been abandoned for ESL (English as a Second Language) teaching that generally focuses on English language proficiency at the expense of bilingualism for nonnative speakers. This is official policy, even though some progressive policymakers are concerned about the continued focus on English in a global economy. In particular, progressives are concerned about the continuing emphasis in U.S. schools on monolingualism, something unheard of in other advanced industrial and postindustrial nations. For the foreseeable future, most teachers will not face homogeneous classrooms of native speakers of English and will need to develop a pedagogy that accounts for this new literacy. In the end, teachers are required to account for and accommodate the linguistic complexity even if the nation pretends that it does not exist.

Classroom Discourse

Once we understand our responsibilities as teachers to comprehend the nature of language and learning as central features of our pedagogy, we then need to look at the specialized functions of language in our teaching and discourse. Firstly, there are two categories of pedagogical discourse: pedagogies of learning and pedagogies of control. The distinction between the two is a particularly troublesome area of discussion. The failure to distinguish between the two is the cause of much wheel spinning in educational debate and, subsequently, in practice. Every school-based lesson has within it a balance between teacher considerations of children learning and children behaving, which are the same thing only in the strictest behaviorist model of human learning.

These two discourses, while essential to one another in discussions of school teaching, are frequently used to attack one another in normal conversation. One teacher talks about teaching methods and is rejected by another who says, "That doesn't work," in most cases meaning that the kids misbehaved during the lesson and would not cooperate. Another attacks college teacher preparation by citing the difficulty new teachers have with classroom management. Teacher educators lament the amount of time spent on discussing classroom control at the expense of learning teaching technique. Another teacher or principal blames the kids for not being "responsible." Although principals want to know whether learning is going on, they are mostly concerned whether you have the classroom under control. It is all intertwined and reciprocal, but these are separate sets of questions and answers.

The most transformative study of the language of classrooms was Arno Bellack et al.'s *Language in the Classroom,* which sought to describe language interaction in real classrooms while dividing the types of language use into categories for the improvement of teaching (1966). Bellack and his colleagues grouped the vast majority of teacher language into four categories:

- Structuring (classroom management and instructional cuing)
- Soliciting (asking questions)
- Reacting (determined by student initiation)
- Responding (thoughtful explanation or clarification)

These categories are helpful for teacher development and even self-assessment when looked at in terms of "interaction analysis," a historically popular way of assessing teacher behavior. A teacher who spends more time on structuring and reacting than soliciting and responding will generally be less effective academically, as will someone who spends no time on structuring and reacting at all. Ideally, a teacher balances all of the language categories, each appropriate to the situation as well as the overall aims. There is always a fluctuating balance in a group setting between managing and instructing.

Bellack's category system provides a way to explain some problems in teacher talk, such as the confusing and generally unwitting use of the rhetorical question. Asking, "Could you all turn to page 25?" confuses the structuring statement, "Turn to page 25" with an expectation tied to soliciting. The problem becomes more obvious when dealing with student behavior: "Do you want me to come over there?" versus "Stop throwing your pencil at Susan."

On the instructional plane, the difference between structuring and soliciting can be the difference between a nebulous instruction, "How would someone develop a formula for a scientific theory?" and a clear expectation, "Give one example of a phenomenon explained by Einstein's theory of relativity." Both are examples of "higher order" question asking (both ask the student to analyze, synthesize, and evaluate), but only the second one is specific and circumscribed. The first is more of a course goal than a classroom question.

The use of the passive voice also causes some confusion in classroom planning, especially when the teacher plans that "a paper will be written" as the goal of the lesson. The planning should be focused on *how* the teacher will teach and *how* the paper will be written, rather than on using magical thinking to expect it to be completed by the students as a result of teaching the content. "A paper will be written" is a structuring comment, an expectation for behavior, but hardly a contribution to the student's learning.

Teacher language can reveal a personal stance or a cultural set of assumptions that are negative influences, such as blaming the kids for a "lack of motivation" or for being "lazy." Those are ad hominem attacks on the kids and are not pedagogically relevant reflection. Even if the student is actually "lazy," based on a false assumption of character traits as inherent, the teacher cannot change the "lazy" part. What we can do is teach the student regardless of the constraints, the student's and ours.

The most illustrative sorts of examples of ineffective classroom discourse seem to have all of the above problems, such as "How do you expect me to grade this paper?" or "What is wrong with you kids?" or "By tomorrow, I want you to have read the next assignment and you will be quizzed on your ability to tell me what the author is saying that you agree or disagree with."

The problem with the Bellack model is the almost exclusive focus on classroom talk. The post-World War II years were the heyday of "question-asking" based on various theories and systems, the most famous of which was Bloom's Taxonomy of Educational Objectives. The taxonomy was based roughly on a developmental thesis that "lower"-level thinking skills were learned first and "higher"-order thinking skills were based on lower-level mental functions. The categories, in hierarchical order, are knowledge, comprehension, application, analysis, synthesis, and evaluation.

The taxonomy gave teachers an order in which to teach (from lower to higher order) and a way of measuring cognitive maturity (did the student exhibit characteristics of "synthesis" in his or her behavior?). Much of the debate about the taxonomy centers on the higher-order functions, analysis, synthesis, and evaluation, with some arguing that evaluation comes before synthesis and some believing that evaluation occurs at all levels. In any case, note that knowledge is at the lowest level of the hierarchy.

Seemingly the only other area of research on teacher discourse (outside of Bellack) in the past century is teacher *question asking*. The obsession with teacher question asking begins in Dewey's time with attempts to inculcate "inquiry" as an approach to teaching students and reaches a crescendo after the publication of Benjamin Bloom's Taxonomy in the 1950s. These hierarchies can be useful for determining what the "level" of a particular question is, mainly as a way to build understanding in the classroom.

For example, the concept of literal and inferential reading and thinking owes much to Bloom. One cannot make appropriate inferences from a text unless one first establishes some literal information from which to infer additional information or interpretation. The purpose of carefully ordering the questions is to teach students how to move from literal information in a text to higher-order thinking about the text. Many teachers begin with the highest-order question first, such as the infamous "What's the author trying to say?" an author's generalization at the top of the abstract thinking scale, or "Do you agree or disagree with the author?" an evaluation question.

Both of these questions should be the goal of a classroom discussion, carefully built upon other relevant information in the text. Neither makes any sense as a first question, and classrooms rightly fall silent in response to such questions (except in advanced classes where the students have already done all of the teacher's work on their own). Is it any wonder that students, faced with this level of abstraction, simply want to know what the teacher wants in the "answer" on the test?

Even in "open" and informal classrooms, the cognitive rationale for question asking centers on teaching higher-order critical and analytical thinking—though the best of these classrooms focus on creative behavior and associative thinking, rather than hierarchies of knowledge and understanding. But, in many cases, higher-order thinking and creative thinking are as much catchall educational slogans as critical thinking, all based on the teacher's ideology rather than on any pedagogical content knowledge. And, given the total focus on the cognitive taxonomy, it would take special training and special commitment to emphasize the creative or aesthetic in any meaningful way.

The language we use to describe teaching is inherited from traditions that may or may not apply to contemporary social conditions (Taylor, 1984). We speak of the literary "canon," a word originally used to describe the approved books of the Bible. We speak of "exposing" the students to literature and culture, or a "rigorous" curriculum—metaphors derived from outdated psychology and Victorian moral tenets. We employ agricultural metaphors ("planting the seed of knowledge and watching it grow," "cultivating minds") to describe social and technological learning activities. We manufacture machine and computer images ("the floppy disks in our heads will fill up," "he has an insufficient data base for problem solving") to describe human cognitive functions. The confusion and imprecision of our curriculum language presents problems for curriculum thinking and discourse, but some of it comes from bias and ignorance. Twenty-five years ago, I attended a lecture by MIT cognitive scientist, linguist, and now best-selling author Stephen Pinker. He said his older colleagues at MIT mocked him for studying "baby talk." Here are the greatest scientific minds of a generation demeaning the study of child language. That attitude seems to debase our culture in ways that are hard to even fathom.

Teacher Narrative and Teacher Voice

One of the key issues for teachers that transcends methodology is "voice." Part of voice is the physical voice itself. Being able to address as many as thirty-four adolescents, or eighteen second-graders, at one time requires a strong voice, both in volume and engagement. Characteristics of a strong voice can include volume, tone, pitch, timbre, and articulation. A loud, angry, screechy, mumbled instruction does not accomplish much in school settings, since the kids first assume you are personally upset with them and, worse, they do not know what you just told them to do. And, of course, confused expectations and adversarial stances lead to all sorts of teaching problems.

Assuming you have worked out the physical elements of voice (take a speech or public speaking class, since these are unaccountably no longer required in teacher preparation), there is the question of one's voice as a teacher. As a teacher, one has a classroom voice, a professional colleague voice, a scholar's voice, and a voice for the rest of the world. Sometimes teachers cannot leave the teacher voice in the classroom. Sometimes we are called upon to be the authority in social settings. English teachers, for example, are always asked to provide the spelling of words or, conversely, to "pardon my grammar" outside of school. Appropriate use of voice and the situational use of grammar or rhetoric are expected of experienced and educated professionals.

The traditional teacher workroom style of discussion tends toward anecdote, of the "you show me, I'll show you" sort, or the "here's how I do it" type. Classroom teachers themselves, especially when targeting professional development inadequacies, sometimes call this approach the "show and tell" model. Another species of school discourse is the "philosophy" statement required for school accreditation agencies, usually high in abstract social goals and quasi-religious sentiments ("Students will learn to be better citizens and attain self-fulfillment through assisting those in need.") and low on curriculum possibilities ("students will engage in complex meaning-making activities within the holistic frame of a diverse linguistic community").

In recent years, a new range of teacher voices has appeared, in the form of teacher narratives. Certainly, there have been teacher narratives throughout history, and also books about students in school that are actually tributes and fictional biographies of great teachers, from *Goodbye, Mr. Chips* to *A Separate Peace.* Most of these books are set in boarding schools, the ultimate *in loco parentis* arrangement, and concern the problems of the future leadership classes. Even the relatively interesting, from a pedagogical perspective, *Dead Poets' Society* is set in a private boarding school. The original of these books was *Tom Brown's School Days,* written by Thomas Hughes in the first half of the 19th century, celebrating England's Rugby School, whose legendary headmaster was Matthew Arnold's father.

The other well-known species of these books are the narratives of "inner-city" teachers, most relevantly begun by Jonathon Kozol's *Death at an Early Age* (1966). These range from serious attempts by earnest young activists to chronicle their experience in urban schools (such as Herbert Kohl in *36 Children*) to pulp trash such as the *Blackboard Jungle,* written by paperback writer Evan Hunter (who is also Ed McBain, the detective fiction writer). The list of new versions of both types, with movie tie-ins, is now endless. Teachers have no interest in any of these books from the perspective of pedagogy because they are not about teaching. Most are simply dramatic situations, and the school the mise-en-scène: the prep school stories are all about making sense of growing up without adult guidance, and the inner city ones are all about taming kids with no parental guidance.

Instead, teachers are interested in the new species of teacher narrative that has become part and parcel of the professional literature. The archetype is Nancy Atwell's *In the Middle,* first published in 1987, a bestseller in educational markets that highlighted actual practice along with Atwell's history of her own development as a teacher. She famously focused on learning *with* her students and providing many examples of student work within the contexts of her various pedagogical discussions. Atwell, of course, was no novice, being a veteran at the time and having completed quite a bit of advanced study. She also worked with a publisher, Robert Boynton, and several professors, including Donald Graves, who were champions of the teacher "voice" in writing and committed to the teacher-researcher vision of the teacher's role. Atwell's book is really about the effect of community, the full community of educators and students, on the teacher's life and work.

Teaching autobiographies, such as *In the Middle,* are very sophisticated versions of the anecdotal model. Sometimes this makes the pedagogy more powerful, and sometimes it adds to the problem. Readers sometimes read these excellent books as "Bibles," books that have no context and no comparable texts. Some teachers used to claim they were "doing Nancy Atwell's process model of writing." That statement shows a complete lack of context, a lack of prior knowledge if you will, regarding composition research and practice at the time.

Mimicking Atwell's classroom practices does not even acknowledge her curriculum frame. It is possible to follow her classroom practice and not have a clue why one is doing it, thereby subverting many of the curricular goals even explicit in Atwell's book. Teachers may adopt some of her terms, such as "mini-lesson" (a confusing and probably unnecessary term), but the technique represents a change in stance and pedagogy that must be understood and employed. In many classrooms, the mini-lesson becomes an abbreviated and limiting introduction to classroom activities. But, Atwell's narrative is so illustrative that those who actually read her book usually did not make that mistake. The narrative itself was stronger in meaning than any codification of the mini-lesson in latter professional development.

Atwell always acknowledges her sources (she certainly does not claim to have invented the process approach to composition) and directs the reader to appropriate resources. She invites teachers to create their own enacted curriculum by drawing on the sources she recommends in the book. Combined with their personal experience, the book could help readers to shape an appropriate curriculum. Atwell's classroom is not a prescription for developing a comprehensive curriculum, but the portrait of a teacher who worked for many years to develop a successful teaching environment.

Many of the teacher narratives that have followed Atwell are simply that—narratives. Some are not only non-reflective but engage in all sorts of irresponsible generalizing about kids and learning and about other teachers for that matter. Simple narratives of experience aimed at a sensationalist best-selling audience do little to help the teaching professional make a case for professionalism, and yet these books continue to make waves in policy situations. Given the very large number of young people engaged in temporary teaching assignments who have great ambitions of the Nanny Diaries type, one can only imagine how many more of these books will appear in the next few years.

There is a complication here as well concerning professional researchers, especially of the behavioral type, who dismiss all teacher narrative as merely "anecdotal" research. Not all teacher narrative is merely narrative, but, by definition, all teacher narrative is "anecdotal." Unfortunately, among scientific researchers, anecdotal research is synonymous with "unprovable." The real argument is over the value, and the place in the context of other research, of teacher voices in research. Much of what one hears regarding the difference between quantitative and qualitative research is about the role of the classroom teacher in the research enterprise.

The question of teacher narrative involves the nature of inquiry, the range of interpretive structures, and the tests of reliability and validity, but it is mostly about "who says?" The value of teacher narrative, separated out from the novels and plays and sensationalism, has already been demonstrated by the history of teaching itself. Ignoring the teachers regarding teaching seems as useful as ignoring doctors on health or ministers on religion. But we do live in a time of the dilettante and the huckster, an age of infotainment and quick fixes. We live in a time of scientific technological certainty and political demagoguery. The trick is in making the voice of the teacher heard above the deafening roar of the new media and the new politics as well as the barking statistics of scientific research.

Words, Texts, and Deeds

Even if teachers are allowed or demand to tell their stories, some of the language that educators use can be ambiguous. Many times we are flailing away, trying to argue for or against nothing more than an educational slogan. An educational slogan is a term that most of us can agree on because it is so abstract that we can all attach our own meanings to it and feel good about it. Educational slogans are always positive, value-laden words. Recently, we have seen the spread of something called "balanced literacy" meant to chart a course between "whole language" and "basal reading/phonics," but each side attaches very different meanings to the phrase.

Everyone is for "democratic education," but what that means could differ wildly from person to person. To some, democratic education means learning the rules of democracy, to others it means learning how to fight hegemonic thinking. Cultural literacy has been rationalized as a democratic necessity, even as it tells people how to be Americans. Every Leftist initiative proclaims, by definition, it is promoting "democratic education" even when it is as deterministic as something like cultural literacy. We all need to beware of easy "solutions" based on sloganeering. After all, who could be against "social justice," but who could agree on a specific program to guarantee it?

Language functions differently in different contexts. Worldview, our cognitive schema, shapes much of our thinking, including language use. What humanists and artists might call "intuitive" or "creative" or "holistic" or some psychologists might call "gestalt" is something that the scientist, especially those in artificial intelligence (AI) research, would call "fuzzy logic." The computer program–modeled vision of thinking in AI research has no place for uncertainty, but sometimes it recognizes that the function of the human brain is not reducible to constituent parts and strictly logical or even algorithmic functions. Rather than accept the language of the humanistic culture, scientists would rather cast the phenomenon in their own terms, in relation to logic. Unfortunately, the ideology of the position is revealed in the attendant reference to fuzzy *thinking* in the humanities and the arts with an implicit pejorative implication. On the other side of the cultural fence, many humanists and artists simply reject any technical language from the sciences as "not getting it," and so whole elements useful to pedagogy are dismissed as anti-humanistic or simply as not artistic. So, English professors rarely study reading or readers, art history professors do not study perception, and students of both domains suffer as result.

Education has frequently, and thoughtlessly, been accused of "reinventing the wheel," a phrase meant to suggest an ahistorical and non-reflective approach to innovation and change. While teaching professionals may be guilty of the charge on occasion, the primary attempts to reinvent the wheel usually arrive as crisis mandates from political or social groups who have a return to a golden age in mind, while camouflaging it as "innovation." In the current confusion, many of the new charter schools and their supporters claim extravagant innovations that are mostly experience-based learning from the Progressive Era or collaborative work on "projects" that date from the same period (e.g., the Dalton Method). Most of the other innovations such as lengthening of the school day and school year, and making the teachers accountable to students 24 hours a day, seven days a week, have little to do with pedagogical innovation (see KIPP Academies, e.g.).

I do not doubt the sincerity or passion of the various reformers, but there is a tendency to blame teachers for all current problems and then put a plan in place that addresses only the administrative issues. There continues to be a sadly mistaken belief among corporate reformers and their politician allies that "managing" the school better administratively, including its "human resources," will result in a more compliant and well-educated population of workers and managers for their businesses. The language of the corporation does not fit the school for good reason.

What one has in that formulation is one of the great paradoxes of schooling for the political and corporate elites: how do you educate people well without making them less controllable? Raymond Williams, the great British sociologist and historian of literacy, remarked that it is impossible to teach a man to read the Bible in a way that prevents him from reading the radical press (*The Long Revolution,* 1975, p. 131). The cruelest comment on the situation of ordinary citizen's education, given the interests of the elites, would be that the conservatives seem to want to deny the poor an education while liberals seem to want to educate the poor to know (and accept) their place. In either world, most U.S. school policy is not about the unlimited human potential of its citizenry.

But educational policymakers and researchers are not always simply "reinventing the wheel," a comment meant to stop discussion of innovation. There is a tendency to start over in educational discussions rather than build on what we have already discovered or decided. But the circle metaphor implicit in the image of the wheel does remind us that things do change even while they appear to stay the same. What goes around comes around, but it is always the same old, same old, as we like to say. Geoffrey Chaucer spoke about the wheel of fate in the 14th century, and the image is as old as human records, so the image is part of our "commonsense" notions of how the world works. If you don't like the weather, wait until tomorrow, is a common comment in almost every region of the United States. What changes is not the basic, the fundamental discussion, but the emphasis within the discussion. We, as a country, keep reinventing the wheel because we continue to have the same disagreements, not because we cannot remember what we are doing.

Politically, power is about who controls the discourse, as George Orwell predicted in his novel *1984* (1949). Right now the neoconservatives (some would say the radical Right) dominate the discourse and control the policies. Therefore, the current emphasis is on:

1. Cultural literacy
2. Core curriculum

3. Essentialism
4. Accountability
5. Scientism
6. Patriotism
7. Privatization
8. Leadership

Given any number of current trends, and historical evidence that cultural shifts will continue to occur, most new teachers will experience another revolution within their career span that will instead emphasize:

1. Multiculturalism
2. Elective curriculum
3. Complexity
4. Responsibility
5. Humanism
6. Reconstructionism
7. Public service
8. Community

It is also likely that the teacher of the near future will be asked by a number of differing constituencies (resulting from an increasingly fragmented and contentious society) to engage in all of the above on both sides, however contradictory. The search for solutions depends on the question. If a person is authorized to ask the question, especially if it as framed and accepted as reflecting a "crisis," that person can control the policy. That crisis mentality determines the possible answers to school "problems" because the person defining the crisis is defining the problem. Someone else asking the same questions will result in another set of "problems" to work on, plus a differing proposal for "solutions."

Speaking of solutions, one must also deal not only with a separation of theory and practice in educational circles, but also with what is frequently and confusingly recast as a "theoretical *versus* practical" argument. The most vulgar version of that discussion is the "what works" framework. There is nothing more practical than a good theory, because all teaching practice is theory-laden. All of our teaching is based on theories of human behavior, theories of thinking, and theories from our subject field.

They can be poor theories or sophisticated theories or limiting theories or radical theories, but no one teaches without a sense of what they plan to do for one purpose or another.

Unfortunately, some people will put this theorizing forward as a "belief," as in, "I believe all kids should do honest work." When it comes to actually acting on that belief, classroom planning and practice need to be recast into a useful theory. For example, "believing" that kids should do "honest" work assumes a cognitive theory about "ownership," a social theory about individual responsibility, and a cultural theory that distinguishes between "true" and "false" knowledge. One could go on.

Just saying that kids should be "authentic" faces the same necessary analysis. What does it mean to be authentic in a mediated world of sampling and animation? Is *authenticity* a criterion that serves educational practice or is it a reactionary stance against modern media culture? In any case, all practice, even the Friday spelling test or subtraction exercises in the second grade, is theory-laden. Even deciding that kids should revise poor work rather than "failing" them is theory laden.

The language of teaching encompasses many different and complex language domains. Classroom discourse is one, educational rhetoric and argument is another, and the language of teaching materials is another. We have already discussed the language of learning and the learning of language. Let's finally address the question of formal language in a *text* as a tool of pedagogy in educational settings.

You are reading a primer. A primer is a pedagogical tool (more like a kaleidoscope than a lens, a favorite ethnographic term, for those thinking "what kind of tool?"). From primers have evolved modern textbooks, representations of cultural knowledge that assist teachers in teaching and students in learning (and sometimes vice versa). Textbooks are part and parcel of the notion of pedagogy (Nietz, 1966). Textbooks exist because of the concept of pedagogy. And, despite the fact that billion of dollars are spent in textbook development and maintenance, they are disposable: no library in America stocks textbooks on its shelves.

Interestingly, the *Ur*-text of America, the first book published in America, is a primer: *The New England Primer* first published in 1688 (Ford, 1897). The *New England Primer* has been cited numerous times over the past several hundred years as the ideal schoolbook. Henry Ford paid to have it, and the McGuffey Readers (textbooks that were primers), reprinted and distributed to schools around the time of World War I. Ford, the original Bill Gates, did so because he believed that American values needed to be defended against the contemporary waves of immigration, and that traditional American schoolbooks provided a vision of American culture appropriate to children who would become the new Americans. (He also seemed to view the word "primer," as in "prim and proper" versus "primer," as an underlying coat of paint, or something meant to start a process, like priming the pump.)

Despite the bad press textbooks receive and the disdain for them that many teachers publicly express, a vast majority of teachers use textbooks because they help us teach students and sometimes remind us of knowledge we learned long ago. Sometimes we learn something for the first time from the textbook. In any case, the textbook is the shared content that the teacher and student focus on in the teaching and learning process. Some textbooks are better than others, and some persist even though everyone complains about them (the decades-long hegemonic hold of Warriner's grammar book in English class comes to mind). But, in the end, textbooks function as a pedagogical tool—they would not exist without the notion of pedagogy.

One of the recurrent debates in the education field is the confusing and probably false distinction between "textbooks" and "source materials." In some fields, the textbook is a source document: literature anthologies are full of stories and poems—in mathematics classes, the textbook is the source content. In other fields, in particular history, the textbook tends to be a historical narrative, the "story" of our past, and students tend to read about events rather than the documents related to those events. Even that has changed in recent years. However, whether we promote a sophisticated textbook approach (a "learning system," as some publishers deem the books plus auxiliary materials) or a source documents approach, both are examples of pedagogical selection and judgment. The discussion over which materials to use always centers on what is appropriate for the learners we teach. That is pedagogical thinking. The text material, in whatever form, has been chosen by the teacher to teach something to the students, even if it is just to "expose" them to the ideas.

Pedagogical thinking is what teachers do; when teachers do not engage in professional thinking, schools become deadly places. Kids know when the teacher is engaged and when the teacher is hoping to get by. One is either a professional or a dilettante, which is not the same as being an expert or a novice in a field. Novice and experts are both professionals, they just have different experiences and different levels of understanding. Pedagogy is the word for professional teaching. Pedagogy is a means to professional dialogue. Pedagogy is the only viable means to the end, the education of children.

Glossary

Linguistic/Psycholinguistic—The study of language is linguistics. The study of language learning and use, and its relationship to thinking, is psycholinguistics, now usually rendered as socio-psycholinguistics to recognize social and cultural influences.

Literacy—The ability to read and write. The definition of literacy changes with the times, and throughout history most of humankind has been illiterate. The test of literacy in the19th century was being able to sign one's name. In the 21st century, nothing short of multimedia literacy will suffice.

Orality—The study of the rules and contexts of spoken language.

Standardization—Establishing agreed upon technical standards in any circumstance or situation. "Fix and ascertain" is an 18th-century expression used by the compiler of the first English dictionary, Dr. Samuel Johnson, to describe his intentions toward the language. The standardized textual form of the language is referred to as "standard written English" (SWE).

Textuality—A postmodern theory situating the object of study as a "text" that is always unfinished and without the possibility of full comprehension. In teaching, it means that there is no answer to the "what's the author trying to say?" question. Textuality also changes the relationship of the reader to the author, and the reader is seen as a socially constructed co-creator of the text. Textuality is also associated with deconstruction, an interpretive and critical stance that seeks to unmask assumptions in texts and expose the contradictions in language.

References

Adler, M. (Ed.). (1983). *The Paideia Program: An Educational Syllabus.* Essays by the Paideia Group. Preface and Introduction by M. J. Adler. New York: Macmillan Publishing.

Adler, M., & Van Doren, C. (1940/1966). *How to Read a Book: The Art of Getting a Liberal Education.* New York: Simon and Schuster.

Adler, M., On Behalf of the Members of the Paideia Group (1982). *The Paideia Proposal: An Educational Manifesto.* New York: Macmillan.

Adler, M. (Ed.) (1990). *Great Books of the Western World* (2nd ed.). Chicago: Encyclopedia Britannica.

Anderson, P. M., & Rubano, G. (1991). *Enhancing Aesthetic Reading and Response.* Urbana, IL: National Council of Teachers of English.

Anderson, P. M., & Summerfield, J. P. (2004). Why is Urban Education Different from Suburban and Rural Education? In S. Steinberg & J. Kincheloe (Eds.), *19 Urban Questions: Teaching in the City*. New York: Peter Lang.

Anyon, J. (2005). *Radical Possibilities: Public Policy, Urban Education, and a New Social Movement.* New York: Routledge.

Apple, M. (1975). The Hidden Curriculum and the Nature of Conflict. In W. Pinar (Ed.) *Curriculum Theorizing: The Re-conceptualists.* New York: McCutchan.

Apple, M. (2004). *Ideology and Curriculum* (3rd ed.). New York: Taylor & Francis.

Arnold, M. (1867). *Culture and Anarchy* (1960 ed.). Cambridge: Cambridge University Press.

Aronowitz, S. (2004). *How Class Works.* New Haven: Yale University Press.

Atwell, N. (1987). *In the Middle: New Understanding about Reading, Writing and Learning.* Portsmouth, NH: Boynton/Cook.

Avildsen, J. (dir.) (1989). *Lean on Me.* Burbank, CA: Warner Brothers.

Barnes, D., Britton, J., & Rosen, H. (1971). *Language, the Learner and the School* (Revised ed.). Baltimore: Penguin Books.

Bass, R. (2008). The Visible Knowledge Project. <http://crossroads.georgetown.edu/vkp/>

Bellack, A., Kliebard, H. M., Hyman, R. T., & Smith, F. L. (1966). *The Language of the Classroom.* New York: Teachers College Press.

Berlin, J. (1987). *Rhetoric and Reality: Writing Instruction in American Colleges, 1900–1985.* Carbondale: Southern Illinois University Press.

Berliner, D. (1986). In Pursuit of the Expert Pedagogue. *Educational Researcher* 15(6), 5–13.

Black, M. (1962). *Models and Metaphors.* Ithaca: Cornell University Press.

Bloom, A. (1987). *The Closing of the American Mind.* New York: Simon and Schuster.

Bloom, B., Englehart, M., Furst, E., Hill, W., & Krathwohl, D. (1956) *Taxonomy of Educational Objectives, Handbook I: The Cognitive Domain.* New York: Longmans Green.

Boyer, E. (1983). *High School: A Report on Secondary Education in America.* New York: Harper and Row.

Brandt, R. (1986). On the Teacher Expert: A Conversation with David Berliner. *Educational Leadership,* 44(2), 4–9.

Britton, J. (1970). *Language and Learning.* Baltimore: Penguin.

Britton, J. (1976). Language and the Nature of Learning: An Individual Perspective. In J. Squire (Ed.), *The Teaching of English* (pp. 1–37). Chicago: University of Chicago Press.

Britton, J., Burgess, T., Martin, N., McLeod, A., & Rosen, H. (1975). *The Development of Writing Abilities* (pp. 11–18). New York: Macmillan.

Brooks, J. (dir.) (1955). *The Blackboard Jungle.* Culver City, CA: MGM.

Bruer, J. T. (1993, Summer). The Mind's Journey from Novice to Expert. *American Educator,* 17(2), 6–15.

Bruner, J. (1985). Narrative and Paradigmatic Modes of Thought. In E. Eisner (Ed.), *Learning and Teaching the Ways of Knowing.* Chicago: University of Chicago Press.

Bruner, J. (1990). *Acts of Meaning.* Cambridge: Harvard University Press.

Bruner, J. (1996). *The Culture of Education.* Cambridge: Harvard University Press.

Callahan, R. (1962). *Education and the Cult of Efficiency.* Chicago: University of Chicago Press.

Cantor, N. (1994). *The Civilization of the Middle Ages: A Completely Revised and Expanded Edition of Medieval History.* New York: Harper Perennial.

Carroll, J. (2007). The Divide between Public School Parents and Private School Parents. *Gallup News Service* (September 5, 2007). <http://www.gallup.com/poll/28603/Divide-Between-Public-School-Parents-Private-School-Parents.aspx>

Cavalli-Sforza, L. (2000). *Genes, Peoples, and Languages.* Berkeley and Los Angeles: University of California Press.

Cheney, L. (1989). *50 Hours: A Core Curriculum for College Students.* Washington, DC: National Endowment for the Humanities.

Cheney, L. V. (1987). *American Memory: A Report on the Humanities in the Nation's Public Schools.* Washington, DC: National Endowment for the Humanities.

Clavell, J. (dir.) (1967). *To Sir with Love.* Hollywood, CA: Columbia Pictures.

Coalition of Essential Schools National Web. <www.essentialschools.org/>.

Cobern, W. W. (2000). *Everyday Thoughts about Nature: A Worldview Investigation of Important Concepts Students Use to Make Sense of Nature with Specific Attention to Science* (Science & Technology Education Library). New York: Springer.

Cole, M. (1996). *Cultural Psychology: A Once and Future Discipline.* Cambridge: Belknap Press of Harvard University Press.

Cole, M., & Scribner, S. (1974). *Culture and Thought.* New York: John Wiley.

Coulter, D., & Wiens, J. (2008). *Why Do We Educate? Renewing the Conversation.* 107th Yearbook of the National Society for the Study of Education. Vol. I. Malden, MA: Blackwell.

Cremin, L. (1964). *The Transformation of the School: Progressivism in American Education 1876–1957.* New York: Vintage.

Darling-Hammond, L., & Bransford, J. (2005). *Preparing Teachers for a Changing World: What Teachers Should Learn and Be Able to Do.* Sponsored by the National Academy of Education. San Francisco: Jossey-Bass.

Davenport, G. (1987). Pergolesi's Dog. *Every Force Evolves a Form: Twenty Essays.* San Francisco: North Point Press.

Dean, C. (2007). James Watson Retires after Racial Remarks. *New York Times* (October 25, 2007). <www.nytimes.com/2007/10/25/science/25cnd-watson.html>

Dewey, J. (1887/1975). *Psychology.* Carbondale: Southern Illinois University Press.

Dewey, J. (1897). My Pedagogic Creed. *The School Journal,* 54(3) (January 16), 77–80.

Dewey, J. (1902). *The Child and the Curriculum.* Chicago: University of Chicago Press.

Dewey, J. (1910/1997). *How We Think.* Mineola, NY: Dover (Expanded edition in 1933.) New York: D. C.

Dixon, J. (1968). *Growth through English.* Urbana, IL: National Council of Teachers of English.

Dussault, R. (2000). Maps and Management: Comstat Evolves. *Government Technology.* <http://www.govtech.com/tt/articles/2163>

Eisner, E. (1979). *The Educational Imagination: On the Design and Evaluation of School Programs.* New York: Macmillan.

Eisner, E. (1985). Aesthetic Modes of Knowing. In E. Eisner (Ed.), *Learning and Teaching the Ways of Knowing.* Chicago: University of Chicago Press.

Eisner, E. W. (1993). Forms of Understanding and the Future of Educational Research. *Educational Researcher,* 22(7), 5–11.

Elyot, T. (1531). *The Boke Named the Governour.* Facsimile edition. London: Scolar Press.

Fennema, E., & Leder, G. C. (Eds.). (1990). *Mathematics and Gender.* New York: Teachers College Press.

Finn, C. (2008). The Thomas B. Fordham Institute. <http://www.edexcellence.net/template/page.cfm?id=126> See also, The State of Alternative Teacher Certification (September 19, 2007). *Inside Higher Education.* <http://www.insidehighered.com/news/2007/09/18/teacher>

Ford, P. L. (Ed.) (1897). *The New England Primer: A History of Its Origin and Development.* New York: Dodd, Mead, & Co,

Freire, P. (1970). *Pedagogy of the Oppressed* (M. B. Ramos, Trans.). New York: Seabury Press.

Freud. S. (1930/2005). *Civilization and Its Discontents.* New York: Norton.

Gardner, H. (1982). *Art, Mind, and Brain: A Cognitive Approach to Creativity.* New York: Basic Books.

Gardner, H. (1993). *Frames of Mind: The Theory of Multiple Intelligences* (10th ed.). New York: Basic Books.

Gee, J. (2004). *Situated Language and Learning: A Critique of Traditional Schooling.* New York: Routledge.

Goodman, K. (1985). Chicago Mastery Learning Reading: 'A Program With Three Left Feet.' *Education Week* (October 9, 1985). <www.edweek.org/ew/articles/1985/10/09/06250017.h05.html>

Gould, S. J. (1996). *The Mismeasure of Man.* New York: W. W. Norton.

Gould, S. J. (2007). *The Richness of Life: The Essential Stephen Jay Gould.* New York: Norton.

Graff, G. (1981). *Beyond the Culture Wars: How Teaching the Conflicts Can Revitalize American Education.* New York: W. W. Norton & Co.

Greene, M. (1981). Aesthetic Literacy in General Education. In J. F. Soltis (Ed.), *Philosophy and Education* (pp. 115–141). Chicago: University of Chicago.

Greene, M. (1988). *The Dialectic of Freedom.* New York: Teachers College Press.

Greene, M. (2000). *Releasing the Imagination: Essays on Education, the Arts, and Social Change.* New York: Jossey-Bass.

Groenig, M. (1987). *School is Hell.* New York: Pantheon.

Grossman, P. (1990). *The Making of a Teacher: Teacher Knowledge and Teacher Education.* New York: Teachers College Press.

Habermas, J. (1970). *Knowledge and Human Interests* (J. Shapiro, Trans.). Boston: Beacon Press.

Habermas, J. (2008). *Between Naturalism and Religion: Philosophical Essays.* (C. Cronin, Trans.). Malden, MA: Polity Press.

Hackford, T. (dir.) (1982). *An Officer and a Gentleman.* Hollywood, CA: Capitol Equipment Leasing.

Hall. G. S. (1908/2004). *Adolescence: Its Psychology and Its Relations to Physiology, Anthropology, Sociology, Sex, Crime, Religion and Education.* Two Volumes. New York: Adamant Media Corp.

Helfand, D. (2000). Researchers Cast Doubt on Texas School "Miracle." *Los Angeles Times* (October 25, 2000). <http://articles.latimes.com/2000/oct/25/news/mn-41714.>

Hemion, D. (dir.) (1992). *The Walt Disney Company Presents the American Teacher Awards.* Los Angeles: Walt Disney Television.

Herrnstein, R., & Murray, C. (1994). *The Bell Curve: Intelligence and Class Structure in American Life.* New York: The Free Press.

Herszenhorn, D. (2006). Teachers' Union Chief Falters in a Pop Quiz on Fractions. *New York Times* (December 28, 2006). <www.nytimes.com/2006/12/28/nyregion/28quiz.html>

Hirsch, E. D., Jr. (1988). *Cultural Literacy: What Every American Needs to Know* (Updated and Expanded ed.). New York: Random House.

Hofstadter, R. (1955). *The Age of Reform: From Bryan to F.D.R.* New York: Random House/Vintage.

Hofstadter, R. (1966). *Anti-Intellectualism in American Life.* New York: Vintage.

Huitt, W. (2003). Models of Teaching/Instruction. *Educational Psychology Interactive.* Valdosta, GA: Valdosta State University. <chiron.valdosta.edu/whuitt/materials/sysmdlo.html>

Hunter, E. (1954). *The Blackboard Jungle*. New York: Simon and Schuster.

Hutchins, R. M. (1952). *The Great Conversation: The Substance of a Liberal Education* (1st ed., Vol. 1). Chicago: Encyclopedia Britannica, Inc.

Irving, W. (1819/1983). The Legend of Sleep Hollow (From the Sketchbook of Geoffrey Crayon, Gent.). (J. Tuttleston, Ed.). *Washington Irving: History, Tales, and Sketches*. New York: Library of America.

Jackson, P. (1968). *Life in Classrooms*. New York: Holt, Rinehart and Winston.

Jacobs, H. H. (Ed.). (1989). *Interdisciplinary Curriculum: Design and Implementation*. Alexandria, VA: Association for Supervision and Curriculum Development.

Jacobs, H. H. (1997). *Mapping the Big Picture: Integrating Curriculum & Assessment, K-12*. Alexandria, VA: Association for Supervision and Curriculum Development.

Jacobs, H. H. (2004). *Getting Results with Curriculum Mapping*. Alexandria, VA: Association for Supervision and Curriculum Development.

Johnson, R. T., & Johnson, D. W. (1986). Action Research: Cooperative Learning in the Science Classroom. *Science and Children* 24, 31–32.

Joyce, B., Weil, M., & Calhoun, E. (2003). *Models of Teaching* (7th ed.). Englewood Cliffs, NJ: Prentice-Hall.

Kaufman, B. (1964). *Up the Down Staircase*. New York: Prentice-Hall.

Kermode, F. (1979). *The Genesis of Secrecy: On the Interpretation of Narrative*. Cambridge: Harvard UP.

Kincheloe, J. L. (2002). *Teachers as Researchers: Qualitative Paths to Empowerment* (2nd ed.). New York: Falmer Press.

Kincheloe, J. L. (2008). *Critical Pedagogy* (2nd ed.). A Peter Lang Primer. New York: Peter Lang.

Kincheloe, J. L., Steinberg, S. R., & Gresson, A. D. (1997). *Measured Lies: The Bell Curve Examined*. New York: St. Martin's Press.

KIPP Academies. <www.kipp.org/> (September 15, 2008).

Klicka, C. (2007). The Myth of Teacher Qualifications. *Current Issue Analysis*. Home School Legal Defense Association. <http://perx.hslda.org/docs/nche/000002/00000214.asp>

Kliebard, H. (2004). *The Struggle for the American Curriculum 1893–1958* (3rd ed.). New York: Routledge.

Kozol, J. (1967). *Death at an Early Age: The Destruction of the Hearts and Minds of Negro Children in the Boston Public Schools*. New York: Bantam.

Kramer, S. (dir.) (1960). *Inherit the Wind*. Hollywood, CA: United Artists.

Krathwohl, D. R., Bloom, B., & Masia, B. (1964). *Taxonomy of Educational Objectives, Handbook II: Affective Domain*. New York: David McKay Co.

Krug, E. (1966). *Salient Dates in American Education, 1635–1964.* New York: Harper & Row.

Kubrik, S. (dir.) (1987). *Full Metal Jacket.* Hollywood, CA: Natant.

Lakoff, G., & Johnson, M. (1980). *Metaphors We Live By.* Chicago: University of Chicago Press.

Langer, S. K. (1953). *Feeling and Form.* New York: Charles Scribner's Sons.

Langer, S. K. (1957). *Philosophy in a New Key.* Cambridge: Harvard University Press.

Lave, J., & Wenger, E. (1991). *Situated Learning: Legitimate Peripheral Participation* (Learning in Doing: Social, Cognitive & Computational Perspectives). Cambridge: Cambridge University Press.

Levin, T., Long, R., & Day, B. (1981). *Effective Instruction.* (B. Bloom preface). Washington, DC: Association for Supervision and Curriculum Development.

McLuhan, M. (1994). *Understanding Media: The Extensions of Man.* Cambridge: MIT Press.

Mansell, W. (2008). No One Wants the Stats Job. *Times Educational Supplement* (August 8, 2008). <http://www.tes.co.uk/2653051>

Michener, J. (1965). *The Source.* New York: Fawcett.

Morton, G. (1994). *The Story of Webster's Third: Philip Gove's Controversial Dictionary and its Critics.* Cambridge: Cambridge University Press.

Mulligan, R. (dir.) (1967) *Up the Down Staircase.* New York: Park Place Productions.

Myers, M. (1985). *The Teacher Researcher: How to Study Writing in the Classroom.* Urbana, IL: ERIC/NCTE.

National Commission on Excellence in Education (1983, April). *A Nation at Risk: The Imperative for Educational Reform* (A Report to the Nation and the Secretary of Education United States Department of Education by The National Commission on Excellence in Education). Washington, USDE. <http://www.ed.gov/pubs/NatAtRisk/risk.html>

Neufeld, M. (2007). *Von Braun: Dreamer of Space, Engineer of War.* New York: Knopf.

Nietz, J. A. (1966). *The Evolution of American Secondary School Textbooks.* Rutland, VT: Charles E. Tuttle Company.

Olson, L. (1989). Texas Restrictions on Teacher Training Cited in Complaint. *Education Week* (March 15, 1989). <www.edweek.org/ew/articles/1989/03/15/08210064.h08.html>

Ong, W. J. (1982). *Orality and Literacy: The Technologizing of the Word.* New York: Routledge.

Orwell, G. (1949). *1984.* London: Secker and Warburg.

Osborn, T. A. (2002). *The Future of Foreign Language Education in the United States.* Westport, Conn. and London: Bergin & Garvey.

Pellegrino, J., Chudowsky, N., & Glaser, R. (Eds.) (2001). *Knowing What Students Know: The Science and Design of Educational Assessment.* National Research Council. Washington, DC: National Academy Press.

Pepper, S. (1970). *World Hypotheses: Prolegomena to Systematic Philosophy and a Complete Survey of Metaphysics.* Berkeley and Los Angeles: University of California Press.

Pinar, W. (Ed.). (1975). *Curriculum Theorizing: The Re-conceptualists.* New York: McCutchan.

Polanyi, M. (1962). *Personal Knowledge.* London: Rutledge, Keegan Paul.

Potter, S. (1937). *The Muse in Chains: A Study in Education.* London: Jonathon Cape.

Pritchett, H. S. (1908). *The Third Annual Report: The Carnegie Foundation for the Advancement of Teaching.* Boston: Merrymount Press.

Purves, A., & Niles, O. (Eds.). (1984). *Becoming Readers in a Complex Society.* Eighty-third Yearbook of the National Society for the Study of Education, Part I. Chicago: University of Chicago Press.

Ravitch, D., & Finn, C. E., Jr. (1988). *What Do Our 17-Year-Olds Know? A Report on the First National Assessment of History and Literature.* New York: Harper & Row/Perennial Library.

Reagan, R. (1986). *Remarks on Receiving the Department of Education Report on Improving Education.* Archives. Ronald Reagan Presidential Library (March 4, 1986). <www.reagan.utexas.edu/archives/speeches/1986/30486b.html>

Reza, H. G. (2004). Bible's Lessons Inspired Initiative. *Los Angeles Times.* (January 12, 2004, B1). <articles.latimes.com/2004/jan/12/local/me-bibleman12>

Richards, I. A. (1929). *Practical Criticism* (Harvest Book ed.). New York: Harcourt, Brace & World, Inc.

Richards, I. A. (1942). *How to Read a Page: A Course in Effective Reading, With an Introduction to a Hundred Great Words.* New York: W. W. Norton.

Ricoeur, P. (1977). *The Rule of Metaphor: Multi-disciplinary Studies in the Creation of Meaning in Language* (R. Czerny, Trans.). Toronto: University of Toronto Press.

Rogers, C. (1961). *On Becoming a Person.* Boston: Houghton Mifflin.

Romer, R., & Fitzgerald, J. (1996). "A Vision for the Role of New Assessments in Standards-Based Reform." In Baron, J. B., & Wolf D. P. (eds.), *Performance-Based Student Assessment: Challenges and Possibilities.* Ninety-Fifth Yearbook of the National Society for the Study of Education, Part I. Chicago: University of Chicago Press.

Rosenblatt, L. (1980 April). What Facts Does This Poem Teach You? *Language Arts,* 57(4), 386–394.

Ross, E. A. (1901). *Social Control: A Survey of the Foundations of Order*. New York: Macmillan.

Rubin, L. (1985). *Artistry in Teaching*. New York: Random House.

Rumelhart, D., & McClelland, J. (1986). *Parallel Distributed Processing: Explorations in the Microstructure of Cognition*. Cambridge: MIT Press.

Scholes, R. (1999). *The Rise and Fall of English: Reconstructing English as a Discipline*. New Haven: Yale University Press.

Schön, D. (1983). *The Reflective Practitioner: How Professionals Think in Action*. New York: Basic Books.

Schubert, W. H. (1986). *Curriculum: Perspective, Paradigm, and Possibility*. New York: Macmillan.

Scott, T. (dir.) (1987). *Top Gun*. Hollywood, CA: Paramount Pictures.

Shannon, P. (1989). *Broken Promises: Reading Instruction in Twentieth-Century America*. Granby, MA: Bergin & Garvey Publishers, Inc.

Shulman, L. (1986). Those Who Understand: Knowledge Growth in Teaching. *Educational Researcher'* 15(2), 4–14.

Shulman, L. (2004). *The Wisdom of Practice: Essays on Teaching, Learning, and Learning to Teach* (Carnegie Foundation for the Advancement of Teaching). San Francisco: Jossey-Bass.

Silberman, C. (1970). *Crisis in the Classroom: The Remaking of American Education*. New York: Random House.

Sizer, T. (1985). *Horace's Compromise: The Dilemma of the American High School* (Updated with a New Afterword by the Author). Boston: Houghton Mifflin Company.

Skinner, B. F. (1948). *Walden Two*. New York: Macmillan.

Slavin, R. E. (1989). Research on Cooperative Learning: An International Perspective. *Scandinavian Journal of Educational Research*. 33(4), 231–243.

Smith, J. N. (dir.) (1995). *Dangerous Minds*. Hollywood, CA: Hollywood Pictures.

Snow, C. P. (1959/1993). *The Two Cultures*. Cambridge: Cambridge University Press.

Stodolsky, S. (1988). *The Subject Matters: Classroom Activity in Social Studies and Mathematics*. Chicago: University of Chicago Press.

Taylor, F. W. (1911). *The Principles of Scientific Management*. New York: Harper Brothers.

Taylor, W. (Ed.) (1984). *Metaphors of Education*. London: Heinemann Educational Books.

Tchudi, S. (1985). *The ABCs of Literacy*. New York: Oxford University Press.

Thorndike, E. L. (1912). *Education: A First Book*. New York: Macmillan.

Thorndike, E. L., & Barnhart, E. (1997). *Thorndike-Barnhart Student Dictionary*. Glenview, IL: Scott, Foresman.

Turner, V. (1974). *Dramas, Fields, and Metaphors: Symbolic Action in Human Society*. Ithaca, NY: Cornell University Press.

Twain, M. (1897). *Following the Equator: A Journey around the World*. New York: Dover.

Tyler, R. (1949). *Basic Principles of Curriculum and Instruction*. Chicago: University of Chicago Press.

US Department of Education. Institute for Educational Sciences. <http://www.ed.gov/about/offices/list/ies/index.html>

US Department of Education. What Works Clearinghouse. <www.whatworks.ed.gov>

Vygotsky, L. (1962). *Thought and Language* (E. Hanfmann & G. Vakar, Trans.). Cambridge: MIT Press.

Weems, M. L. (1800). *The Life and Memorable Actions of George Washington*. Philadelphia: By the Author.

Weiner, N. (1967). *The Human Use of Human Beings: Cybernetics and Society*. New York: Avon Books.

Wells, S. (2002). *The Journey of Man: A Genetic Odyssey*. New York: Random House.

Wenger, E. (1999). *Communities of Practice: Learning, Meaning and Identity*. Cambridge: Cambridge University Press.

Wiggins, G. P. (1999). *Assessing Student Performance: Exploring the Purpose and Limits of Testing*. San Francisco: Jossey-Bass Publishers.

Williams, R. (1975). *The Long Revolution*. New York: Greenwood Press.

Willinsky, J. (1990). *The New Literacy: Redefining Reading and Writing in the Schools*. New York: Routledge.

Willis, P. (1981). *Learning to Labor: How Working Class Kids Get Working Class Jobs*. New York: Columbia University Press.

Wilson, E. O. (1998). *Consilience: The Unity of Knowledge*. New York: Vintage.

Zaks, A. J. III (2001). *The Poetics of Rock: Cutting Tracks, Making Records*. Berkeley and Los Angeles: University of California Press.

Index

Peter Lang PRIMERS
in Education

Peter Lang Primers are designed to provide a brief and concise introduction or supplement to specific topics in education. Although sophisticated in content, these primers are written in an accessible style, making them perfect for undergraduate and graduate classroom use. Each volume includes a glossary of key terms and a References and Resources section.

Other published and forthcoming volumes cover such topics as:

- Standards
- Popular Culture
- Critical Pedagogy
- Literacy
- Higher Education
- John Dewey
- Feminist Theory and Education
- Studying Urban Youth Culture
- Multiculturalism through Postformalism
- Creative Problem Solving
- Teaching the Holocaust
- Piaget and Education
- Deleuze and Education
- Foucault and Education